D0291514

# A TEXAS COWBOY

DISCARD

A BISON
BOOK

# A TEXAS

## WITH BIBLIOGRAPHICAL STUDY &
### INCLUDING ADDENDA TO THE 1886 EDITION

TYPOGRAPHY BY CARL HERTZOG

# COWBOY

*OR FIFTEEN YEARS ON THE HURRICANE DECK*
*OF A SPANISH PONY ~ TAKEN FROM REAL LIFE BY*

## CHARLES A. SIRINGO

## INTRODUCTION BY J. FRANK DOBIE

*AND DRAWINGS BY TOM LEA*

UNIVERSITY OF NEBRASKA PRESS
LINCOLN AND LONDON

Copyright © 1950 by William Sloane Associates
Copyright © 1979 by the University of Nebraska Press
All rights reserved
Manufactured in the United States of America
Library of Congress Catalog Card Number 79–63094
International Standard Book Number 0–8032–9111–6

*First Bison Book printing: 1979*

*Most recent printing indicated by first digit below:*
　 2　　3　　4　　5　　6　　7　　8　　9　　10

*The introduction, bibliography, text, and illustrations of this edition are
reprinted by arrangement with William Morrow & Company, Inc. (in
behalf of William Sloane Associates, Inc.) The Addenda are reprinted from
a copy of the 1886 edition in the Western Americana Collection of The
Beinecke Rare Book and Manuscript Library, Yale University Library.*

# CONTENTS

# ILLUSTRATIONS

# INTRODUCTION

# CHARLIE SIRINGO, WRITER AND MAN

## By J. FRANK DOBIE

CHARLES A. SIRINGO was born in Matagorda County, Texas, February 7, 1855, and he died in Hollywood, California, October 19, 1928. Angelo Siringo, the census report of 1860 has the name; he was known to thousands simply as Charlie Siringo. For the first eleven years of his life he was his "folk's contrary son." For the next fifteen years or so he was a cowboy; then, for two decades, a detective. Thereafter his life, lived mostly in New Mexico and California, was meager and splattered, some of it spent in writing, perhaps more of it spent in contesting a power that suppressed what he had written. Carrying them in a satchel, he peddled his own privately printed books.

He wrote his first book when he was less than thirty years old but was considering himself "an old stove-up cowpuncher." It is the story of his life on the range. During the last twenty years or so of his life he repeatedly rewrote the story, with the additions made by time but without those extensions in meaning that an expanding intellect gives to a subject on which it prolongs consideration. His second book, however, is independent of the first, beginning with his employment as a private detective in Chicago in 1886. Two years before this a blind phrenologist who came to Caldwell, Kansas, had felt his "mule head" and assured him that he was "cut out for a detective." His titles in order of publication are: *A Texas Cowboy* (1885), *A Cowboy Detective* (1912), *Two Evil Isms: Pinkertonism and Anarchism* (1915),

*A Lone Star Cowboy* (1919), *Billy the Kid* (1920), *Riata and Spurs* (1927). Siringo had five themes: his experience on the range; Billy the Kid, whom he chased as a cowboy; Pinkerton's National Detective Agency, for which he worked for twenty-two years; tough men and tough experiences that he met as a detective; and then more tough men. He had an inclination to write about women but suppressed it. Whatever he might have said on the subject would not have been news. His collection of cowboy songs is hardly to be rated as a book.

The first book of any significance pertaining to the range, *Historic Sketches of the Cattle Trade of the West and Southwest*, by Joseph G. McCoy, appeared in 1874. In point of time, Siringo's *A Texas Cowboy, or Fifteen Years on the Hurricane Deck of a Spanish Pony* was the second range book of any significance to appear. The next landmarks, in time, are Owen Wister's *The Virginian* (1902) and *The Log of a Cowboy*, by Andy Adams (1903). Since the beginning of the century many valid books, historical, semi-fictional, biographical and autobiographical have been added to the literature of the range.

Siringo was not only the first authentic cowboy to publish an autobiography; of all cowboys, both spurious and authentic, who have recollected in print he was the most prolific in autobiographic variations. No record of cowboy life has supplanted his rollicky, reckless, realistic chronicle. The nearest competitor in the qualities mentioned is *We Pointed Them North*, by Teddy Blue (E. C.) Abbott, put into writing by Helena Huntington Smith. This book tells more about a cowboy's private life with public women and is far better written, but it and all other cowboy reminiscences, including Siringo's own retellings, are supplements to the initial autobiography.

"Dear Charley," Will Rogers wrote to Siringo—and Siringo printed the letter on a self-addressed postcard to be filled out with an order for his *Riata and Spurs*—"Dear Charley: Somebody gave me the proof sheet of your new book, 'Riata and Spurs,' and wanted to know what I think of it. What I think of it? I think the same of it as I do the first cowboy book I ever read, 'Fifteen Years on the Hurricane Deck of a Spanish Pony.' Why, that was the Cowboy's Bible when I was growing up. I camped with a herd one night at the old LX Ranch, just north of Amarillo in '98, and they showed me an old forked tree where some old bronc had bucked you into. Why, that to us was like looking at the Shrine of Shakespeare to some of these 'deep foreheads.' . . . If you live to be a thousand years old you couldn't write a bad book about the Cowboys—the stuff they did might be bad, but you could tell it so well it would sound almost respectable."

The virtue of *Fifteen Years on the Hurricane Deck of a Spanish Pony* is that it was written and published without benefit of respectability. There is, in truth, something incongruous in the present artistic reprint of it, with this sophisticated essay appended. The bibliographical history of the book justifies calling it "the cowboys' Bible."

The first edition, cloth-bound, "Copyrighted by Chas. A. Siringo, Caldwell, Kans.," without date, bears the imprint of M. Umbdenstock & Co., Publishers, Chicago, Illinois, 1885. This edition, now scarcer than hen's teeth, was very limited. The second edition, also in cloth, printed without allusion to the first, "Copyrighted by Charles A. Siringo, 1886," appeared under the imprint of Siringo & Dobson, Publishers, Chicago, Ill., 1886. Through page 316 it is identical with the first edition, except for lack of one of the two colored frontispieces and for the change in publisher's name on the title page. But this second edition has thirty-one pages of "Addenda," an "Index to Addenda," and a dedication. The Addenda tells how to get rich and go broke in the cattle business and gives an unvarnished account of how brutish cowboys treat their horses.

About the time it was published, Siringo moved to Chicago, thence to ride the hurricane deck of his literary pony over a long and crooked trail. The date of the next publication of the book is difficult to fix. In 1893, using the original plates, but without colored frontispiece, The Eagle Publishing Company of Chicago brought out a cloth-bound edition. On the back strip of the binding of my copy of this printing, the name Rand McNally and Co. is stamped in gold. Judging from advertisements in the back of the book, The Eagle Publishing Company was a subsidiary. Carl Hertzog of El Paso owns a paper-bound copy of the book, issued by Rand, McNally and Company, Chicago, that, though undated, he is certain was issued prior to the 1893 printing, certain letters showing the type to have been less worn, or "broken." This printing reproduces both colored illustrations of the 1885 edition. Before long, Rand, McNally & Co. issued the book, using the original plates, as No. 56 in their Globe Library series.

In answer to a query, on August 16, 1935, Mr. B. B. Harvey, editor of the publishing division of the company, wrote me: "Our records date back only to 1901. Between that year and 1912, when our publication of the book was discontinued, we printed 98,000 copies." Presumably, the company printed many thousands of copies before 1901.

They were paper-backed and were sold by butcher boys on trains. Some day the history of butcher boys as purveyors of literature should be written. The butcher boys were not to be deprived of one of their best sellers by Rand, McNally & Company's dropping it from their list. In 1914 copyright on it expired. Immediately thereafter the J. S. Ogilvie Publishing Company of 57 Rose Street, New York, had the book set up in small font type, printed on rotten paper with very narrow margins, bound in paper, and placed on sale at thirty-five cents a copy. At the back of this printing is added a six-page "Publisher's

*Chromo lithograph frontispiece of first edition (not in second edition).*
*Used later as front cover of butcher-boy editions.*

*Second frontispiece of first edition and only frontispiece of second edition. Used as back cover of butcher-boy editions.*

Note" calculated to inspire young men to travel on railroads to the Texas Panhandle to become cowboys. According to a letter from the company dated June 28, 1935, between 1914 and 1926, when the book was dropped from their list, they "printed and sold 58,000 copies."

In 1915 Siringo published the statement, in *Two Evil Isms*, that copies of the book "up into the hundreds of thousands" had been sold. In 1919 he prefaced *A Lone Star Cowboy* with these words: "This volume is to take the place of 'A Texas Cowboy,' the copyright of which has expired. Since its first publication, in 1885, nearly a million copies have been sold."

During a drouth and die-up of the eighties—before government aid to suffering citizens became popular—some farm and ranch people in Jack County, Texas, gathered together to pray for rain and, in case it didn't rain, for supplies from the charitably inclined. Most provisions in those days came in barrels and were sold to ranches by the barrel. "Oh, God," an old cowman prayed, getting louder and higher as he proceeded, "soften the hearts of people in the East to send us according to our needs. Put it into their hearts to send us barrels of flour, barrels of lard, barrels of coffee, barrels of meal, barrels of salt pork, barrels of beans, barrels of molasses, barrels of sugar, barrels of vinegar, barrels of salt, barrels of pepper, barrels——." Just at this point his plea was broken into by an elbow against his ribs and a rough whisper, "Oh, hell, that's too much pepper."

"Nearly a million copies" of *A Texas Cowboy* is probably too much pepper. Range people have never been the chief consumers of any widely distributed book. *A Texas Cowboy* was widely distributed during forty years, under the imprint of five different publishers, and it is safe to say that, along with many readers who clerked in city stores and wanted to be cowboys, most men of the ranges who read at all read it. Many a ranch hand who had ridden a cattle train to Kansas City, Omaha, Chicago or some other market and then came back home in a chair car bought a copy of Charlie Siringo's book from the butcher boy—provided also with *The Ashes of Love, Why Women Sin, A Wounded Heart, The Unmarried Mother, Custer's Last Fight,* and *Anna Karenina,* by Count Leo Tolstoi. Whatever the total number of copies printed, *A Texas Cowboy* has been, by far, Siringo's most-read book, also the most-read non-fiction book on cowboy life.

When Siringo rewrote the story of his boyhood and early manhood under the title of *A Lone Star Cowboy,* he left out many vivid incidents and cow camp phrases. It was this polited version that he transferred into *Riata and Spurs.* He had grown more cautious, and he seemed to have the idea that the public would be more interested in bad men than in his own personal experiences. Whisky-peet, or Whisky-peat—under either spelling a mighty tough pony—seems to have more vitality than the Whisky Pete in the print of a Boston publisher. In *A Texas Cowboy* the dew is on the vine and vitality is uncurbed by correctness, discretion, decorum and other respectabilities. The young cowboy rides "with his head thrown back and a-singing a song." Instead of rashly writing down his own rashness, as he had done at thirty, Siringo, past sixty, in a field no longer "untrodden," was reviewing the rashness of another man. While he never lost altogether his youthful buoyancy, he did not possess that combination of spirit and imagination which for some men and women the years only enrich. Hudson at eighty put a richness into the story of his own Far Away and Long Ago youth that he could never have achieved while riding the pampas—on a Spanish cow pony that differed from Siringo's in surface brand rather than in breed.

*Riata and Spurs* is the meatier book, its parts more amply filled out, but Siringo the Elder makes no such quick judgments as in youth he made on certain cattle kings: " 'Shanghai' Pierce and his brother Jonathan had sold out their interests . . . for the snug little sum of one hundred and ten thousand dollars. That shows what could be done in those days, with no capital, but with lots of cheek and a branding iron. The two Pierce's had come out there from Yankeedom a few years before poorer than skimmed milk. . . . Mr. Grimes had a slaughter house on his ranch where he killed cattle for their hides and tallow—the meat he threw to the hogs. . . . Did you ask kind reader, if those were all his own cattle that he butchered? If so, will have to say that I never tell tales out of school."

Let us compare an account in (1) *A Texas Cowboy* with one of the same incident in (2) *Riata and Spurs*.

(1) "An old irishman by the name of 'Hunky-dorey' Brown kept the store and did the settling up with the men. When he settled with me he laid all the money, in silver dollars, that I had earned since commencing work, which amounted to a few hundred dollars, out on the counter and then after eyeing me awhile, said: 'Allen, Pool & Co. owe you three hundred dollars,' or whatever the amount was, 'and you owe Allen, Pool & Co. two hundred ninety-nine dollars and a quarter, which leaves you seventy-five cents.' He then raked all but six bits into the money drawer. . . . I thought the whole pile was mine and therefore had been figuring on the many purchases that I intended making. My intentions were to buy a herd of ponies and go to speculating. I had a dozen or two ponies, that I knew were for sale, already picked out. . . . After pocketing my six bits, I mounted 'Fannie,' a little mare that I had bought not long before, and struck out."

(2) "I had been working for the Rancho Grande Company nearly two years, without a settlement or knowing how my account in the company store stood. My wages were twenty dollars a month, and whenever I needed cash all I had to do was ask old Hunkey Dory Brown, who was in charge of the store, for the amount, and he would charge it to my account. I was a sur-

prised and disappointed boy when I found out I had only seventy-five cents to my credit. This I blew in for a bottle of peaches and brandy and some stick candy before leaving the store to ride away on my own pony."

The latter account reports the incident in a spirited manner. The earlier one, to use a phrase out of an old cowboy toast, pictures it with a "glow and a glee."

That toast seems to belong here. An old trail-driver who knew Charlie Siringo taught it to me in San Antonio the very day that Siringo died. We were in an upper chamber of a hotel, trail drivers milling in the lobby below us and dancing to the music of three fiddlers. I remember the date from the fact that on the train home next day I read in a newspaper an account of Siringo's death. The toast must be recited with eyes fixed on a glass of red likker held out in the right hand:

*Here's to the vinagaroon that jumped on the centipede's back,*
*He looked at him with a glow and a glee,*
*And he said, "You poisonous son-of-a-bitch,*
*If I don't get you, you'll get me."*

Well, God save us all from ever becoming wholly discreet.

Degrees of honesty are observable in all human expression, but nowhere more patent than in autobiographic writing. The nearest to zero in honesty that any autobiography pertaining to the range has reached is Frank Harris' *My Reminiscences as a Cowboy,* a book significant for its worthlessness. Charlie Siringo never pretends; he is as free from trying to make effects as any man who writes about himself can be. His ignorance of rhetoric and his indifference to what appeals to the public were aids to honesty. From the first form in which he set down his experiences until the final form, he remained uninfluenced by the feeling of most writers on the West that they must raise thunder over oceans of blood. He specialized in bad men, but their gunmanship is never theatrical. His style, especially his early style, cannot be called dignified, but it is informed with the innate dignity of honesty.

One coldish, misty December day, towards sundown, in the year 1931, I rode up to a ranch house on the San Bernard River, in Brazoria County, Texas. A white man of advanced years was out in a pen with three Negro cowboys. One of them, hatless and gray-headed, had matches curled up in his kinky hair. The smoke from his pipe was mingling with the steam from a sweaty horse he was unsaddling. I meant to ask the white man about that way of carrying matches, but when he told me that his name was Jim Keller [1] I remembered that Charlie Siringo had spoken of a Jim Keller who once loaned him a saddle horse. This was the man. We went inside the house to drink coffee and talk. Somehow what he told me lit up the Charlie Siringo of mavericks, mustangs, mossy-horned steers, fenceless coastal ranges, hide and tallow factories and Shanghai Pierce's bellowing voice more than anything else I have met outside of Siringo's first autobiography.

Keller had known Siringo as a boy and worked with him on Grimes' Rancho Grande. "His father was Italian and his mother's name was Bridget. He was happy-go-lucky and usually out of luck. He could let more horses get away with the saddle on than any other cowboy in the country. That first book of his told things just like they was."

Keller said Siringo was the most fearless and the coolest man he ever knew. One time on a cow-work Siringo and a cowboy named Otto had a quarrel. Soon afterwards Siringo was in camp squatted down on the ground eating dinner when Otto suddenly called out to him from behind, "Charlie, I'm going to kill you. Don't move."

[1] James W. Keller, 1850-1946.

Siringo turned his head just enough to see the barrel of a six-shooter.

"All right," he said, not interrupting eating on a calf rib, "but I have a favor to ask before I die."

"What is it?"

"You've heard me say more than once that I hoped I'd not die hungry. I dread dying on an empty belly."

Without saying anything but still holding his six-shooter on the target, Otto apparently agreed to let Charlie finish his last meal. Charlie did not seem to slow down the process of filling up on beans, calf ribs and skillet bread in order to put off the act of dying.

"And I have another favor to ask," Charlie went on, his back to Otto, his squatting position unshifted.

"What's that?"

"When you shoot, don't quit till you've killed me dead. Don't just wound me and leave me wallering around to bother other people. Even if you have to reload to finish me, keep on shooting."

Meanwhile, out of Otto's sight, Charlie's hand was deftly working towards his own six-shooter, which he wore frontward. In a flash it was out and Charlie whirled around, covering Otto.

"Otto," he called, "put that gun up. It might go off and shoot a horse or something. Put it up and eat your dinner."

Otto put it up and ate his dinner. As Jim Keller concluded the story, "A man's wrath cools on a full stomach."

Nobody would ever classify Siringo as an intellectual, but he had one quality of the thorough intellectual—freedom from sentimentality. As their songs, frequently wailing through calf slobber, testify, cowboys in general were inclined to be sentimental. Charlie Siringo certainly had affections, but his emotions were always controlled. May D. Rhodes heard him tell Gene Rhodes that he deserved no credit for the bravery attributed to him, that he was born without a sense of fear.

Without sentiment, he related experiences with a concrete fidelity and a remarkable economy, often with a quick humor and, especially in early years, with lightheartedness. Although he had a strong sense of justice, he was generally as objective towards the criminals he spent so many years pursuing as he was towards some stray cow shot down for her hide. He seems, for instance, to have cared not at all whether Billy the Kid, who pervades his narratives, was captured or not. Probably he sympathized with him.[2]

What urged Siringo to write the story of a cowboy's life, and then to go on and on rewriting it? It was not that "obscure, inner necessity" that Conrad felt driving him on. Siringo was not, like Thoreau, trying to "drive life into a corner" and squeeze out its meaning. He seldom so much as alluded to the realities within himself. As a writer he ignored those passions, those searchings for something essential, those vague yearnings, fears and hidings, those dreams that lie dormant and that smoulder and surge deep within the intelligent being. He wrote down only what a camera or a public stenographer might record. He recorded what the eyes and the memory of a first-class detective gave him. A large proportion of his books have to do with crime and violence, but it would never have occurred to him to speculate on "Murder as

[2] The happy-go-lucky, improvident, haphazard expedition after Billy the Kid has more than anything else that he wrote about put Siringo's name into books—books that go on mulling over the career of "the Robin Hood of New Mexico." In literary qualities, most of this literature approaches the old Robin Hood ballads and folk tales about as nearly as some self-advertised "Athens of Texas" approaches the Athens of Pericles and Socrates.

The best man who rode with Siringo after Billy the Kid was Jim East. The clearest and most orderly account of the expedition to be found is in an essay by J. Evetts Haley: "Jim East—Trail Hand and Cowboy," in the *Panhandle Plains Historical Review*, Canyon, Texas, Vol. IV (1931). Haley also contributed a compact biography of Siringo to the *Dictionary of American Biography*.

a Fine Art." The stuff of poetry, "emotion recollected in tranquillity," did not enter his reminiscences. He was singularly wanting in sensitiveness to the beautiful.

The most original pages Siringo ever published are the three that compose the preface to *A Texas Cowboy.* Playfully, but none the less truthfully, he there tells why he wrote not only this book but all the simulacra that followed: "Money—and lots of it."

In this preface—as original but not so blatant as David Crockett's preface to his autobiography—Siringo specifies the exact experience that set him to hunting and then to writing about an "untrodden field." It was the *Police Gazette,* imposed on a cow camp by two young Texans who could read only the pictures. The one other literary allusion that I have noticed in Siringo's writings is to "a finely-bound novel" that Billy the Kid gave him in exchange for a cigar-holder. He particularized on the "new ten-dollar cigar-holder," but leaves the novel as unidentified as the songs the sirens sang to Ulysses. In April, 1940, Dawson's Book Shop, one of the most civilized institutions of Los Angeles, issued a catalogue listing sixteen books from Siringo's "Den." They are nearly all old acquaintances of mine—John W. Poe's *Billy the Kid,* J. L. Hill's *The End of the Cattle Trail,* Frank S. Millard's *A Cowpuncher of the Pecos*—for which I got the printer not to change spelling, punctuation or sentence structure. Not one of the sixteen books could be classed as literature in the restricted sense of the word.

Siringo was educated to the extent of being able to "read, write and recollect." Had his mind been permeated with the essence of literature, he would not have been the representative that he was of cowboys bookless and booted who rode so free over the free ranges. Agnes Morley Cleaveland, in her delightful *No Life for a Lady,* quotes a cowboy as saying, "I never read a-tall, 'cept when I don't want to think, which ain't often." But even non-reading cowboys, as a part of vacuum-abhoring nature, sometimes craved printed words. In the absence of something else, they not only read but memorized and recited the printing on tin can labels, sometimes arguing whether ozs. should be pronounced "ozzes" or "ounces." In *The Log of a Cowboy*, Andy Adams pictures such a literary session after supper one evening on the cattle trail to Montana.

"Bob Blades toyed with the empty can in mingled admiration and disgust over a picture on the paper label. It was a supper scene, every figure wearing full dress. 'Now that's General Grant,' he said, pointing with his finger, 'and this is Tom Ochiltree. I can't quite make out this other duck, but I reckon he's some big auger—a senator or governor, maybe. Them old girls have got their gall with them. That style of dress is what you call *lo* and *behold*. The whole passel ought to be ashamed. And they seem to be enjoying themselves, too.' "

Many a cow hand batching alone in some ranch outpost, a wooden shack or a dugout, was educated as to what the world was buying and using by a mail-order catalogue. After the big catalogues began circulating widely, they were probably read on the ranges more eagerly than the Bible was.

One cowboy of open-range days used to say that the most satisfactory reading he had ever done was in an abandoned nester's shack where he spent the winter. The nester's wife had papered the walls and ceiling of the one room with pages from a semiweekly newspaper and a farm journal. This cowboy started in on the south wall and read in turn the east, west and north walls and was well along on the ceiling when word from headquarters came for him to join the spring roundup.

While camping in the Cherokee Strip of Oklahoma about 1880, Dennis Collins, a beef buyer, sent his solitary helper to Dodge City on an eight- or ten-day trip with "strict orders not to forget to bring something to read." There was nothing readable at hand, Dennis Collins wrote long afterwards, "except a patent medicine pamphlet, and I had read that so often and so thoroughly that I had some of the symptoms of seven different maladies that were therein pronounced fatal. If I had been in the neighborhood of a drug store at the time, I should have bought a supply of the cure-all, regardless of results." [3]

Granville Stuart, who of all chroniclers among pioneer cowmen had perhaps the most richly-stored mind, tells in his *Forty Years on the Frontier* a graphic story of book-hunger. This was in 1860, twenty years before the library of his Montana ranch home was stocked with three thousand books, along with magazines and newspapers, all at the disposal of range men.

"My brother James and I were both great readers," he wrote, "and we had been all winter without so much as an almanac to look at. We were famished for something to read when some Indians from the Bitter Root told us that a white man had come up from below with a trunk full of books and was camped with all that wealth in Bitter Root valley. On receipt of these glad tidings, we saddled our horses and, putting our blankets and some dried meat for food on a pack horse, started for those books, a hundred and fifty miles away, without a house or anybody on the route and with three dangerous rivers to cross, the Big Blackfoot, the Hell Gate, and the Bitter Root. As the spring rise had not yet begun, by careful searchings we found fords on these rivers, but they were dangerous and at times we were almost swept away.

"Arriving in the Bitter Root valley, we learned that the man who brought the books had gone back to the lower country but had left the precious trunk in charge of a man named Henry Brooks. We finally found him living in a tepee on Sweathouse Creek. We gradually and diplomatically approached the subject

[3] Dennis Collins, *The Indians' Last Fight, or the Dull Knife Raid* (Girard, Kansas: Press of the Appeal to Reason, n.d.), p. 103.

of books, and 'our hearts were on the ground' when Brooks told us that Neil McArthur, a Hudson's Bay Company trader, who left the books in his care, told him to keep them until he returned. He gave him no authority to sell any of them. We told him how long we had been without anything to read and how we had ridden many days, seeking that trunk, and that we would take all the blame and would make good with McArthur when he returned. At last we won him over, and he agreed to let us have five books, for five dollars each, and if McArthur was not satisfied we were to pay him more.

"How we feasted our eyes on those books! We could hardly make up our minds which ones to choose, but we finally settled upon Shakespeare and Byron, both fine illustrated editions, Headley's *Napoleon and his Marshals,* a Bible in French, and Adam Smith's *Wealth of Nations.* After paying for them we had just twenty-five dollars left, but then we had the blessed books, which we packed carefully in our blankets, and joyfully started on our return ride of a hundred and fifty miles. Many were the happy hours we spent reading those books, and I have them yet [about fifty years later]—all except the *Wealth of Nations,* which, being loose in the binding, has gradually disappeared until only a few fragments remain. McArthur never returned to the Bitter Root valley, and I do not know what became of the rest of the books, but I do hope they gave as much pleasure to some others as did the five to Brother James and myself."

One of Granville Stuart's fellow-cowmen didn't think much of his passion for books. He bought a herd of cattle, as he told, from Stuart to be delivered across country at the railroad. Both buyer and seller went with the herd. "Granville was always a great hand to read. He thought it would be a good thing to take a lot of books along for cowpuncher enjoyment. Darned if I know how many he had, but anyway a sackful. The way those cowboys would tackle the books was a caution. They would ride into camp and pick up a book and the cook could holler 'Grub Pile' till he was red in the face and never get all of them to eat at the same time. As soon as one cowboy dropped a book, another would grab it. The cook called me aside one day and told me he was going to quit as the boys thought more of Granville's books than they did of his grub. It would not do to lose a good cook on the trail. I told him not to say anything and I would see that the books caused him no more trouble. The next day when we got to the Yellowstone, I gathered up the books and threw them into the river, thus starting the first circulating library in Montana." [4]

There were not many cowboys like John W. Kendrick, who became Wyoming's best-known senator and who, while the rest of the cowboys were playing poker, "was always to be found in his bunk with a book in his hand." The outstanding cowboy reader was Eugene Manlove Rhodes. He read not only in camp but on horseback, habitually carrying a book in saddle pocket or coat pocket. His fictional cowboys are as apt as he was in literary allusion, and in *Bransford in Arcadia* he explains this aptitude by saying that all cowboys smoked Bull Durham tobacco, got from each sack of tobacco a coupon valid for one paper-bound book, and sent for the books. There were "three hundred and three" titles on the list, most of them classics, since not being copyrighted makes classics cheap. "The books were read," Gene Rhodes says.

Rhodes lived in New Mexico, but there were far more reading men on the ranges of the Northwest than of the Southwest. More young men with cultural backgrounds from New England, England and Scotland went to Montana, Wyoming and the Dakotas to ranch than to Texas and other parts of the Southwest. "Frank and I have gone in for a course in Shakespeare this winter . . . but Jem sticks to his Tennyson and such lighter stuff," wrote

[4] A. J. Noyes, *In the Land of the Chinook, or The Story of Blaine County* (Helena, Montana, 1917), p. 50.

"I. R." in a little-known little book entitled *A Lady's Ranche Life in Montana* (London, 1887). Frank had been in the West sometime, but as a bride I. R. and her Jem had just come over from Kensington Gardens. One of Frank's literary experiences in the country would have been utterly foreign to the Staked Plains or the Mexican borders.

Riding alone on a horse-buying expedition, he was arrested by vigilantes for a horsethief and taken to a cow camp, the cowboys of which at once prepared to hang him. He protested his innocence, but evidence was incontrovertible that his horse was of the size and color ridden by a thief known to be on the dodge. A well-educated man among the vigilantes took the lead in cross-examining him.

"Where were you in 1881?" he asked.

"In Canada."

"Where were you in 1880?"

"In Montana."

"Well, where were you in 1879?"

"In Oxford University."

A derisive cheer followed this reply. He was weather-tanned and unshaven and wore rough clothes. "Tell that to the marines," came calls.

"I'm telling you. Give me time and I can prove it," Frank said.

The cross-examiner went on. "All right, name some authors you studied in Oxford."

"Livy, Virgil, Homer, Aeschylus, Euripides and . . ."

The looks on the faces of the committee were changing. Breaking into the roll call, the cross-examiner said, "Quote some Latin and you are a free man."

"Propria quae maribus," he began and then translated the Latin into Greek. He was a free man.

Philip Ashton Rollins, whose *The Cowboy* is the fullest exposition on the subject printed, whose magnificent collection of Western books and pamphlets, including saddle catalogues, has been presented to Princeton University, and who will go to his grave a romantic, said:

"The Englishmen brought a lot of culture into the West. There were practically no books out there, but an Englishman always brought Shakespeare with him: it was the decent thing to do. And they read their books, read them aloud to the cowboys, many of whom never got any further in their schooling than the rudiments of reading and writing. I've seen a bunch of cowboys sitting on their spurs listening with absolute silence and concentration while somebody read aloud. . . . Once when something of Oscar Wilde's was being read, one of the cowboys got up and left the room. Later I asked him why, and he said, 'I don't see no beauty in watching a hog eat swill.' And I remember once after we'd been listening to *Julius Caesar,* one of them said to me, 'That Shakespeare is the only poet I've ever heard who was fed on raw meat.' When I sold my ranch in Montana, I divided my books among the riders, and eighteen out of twenty-one wanted Shakespeare. I sent out fifteen sets of Shakespeare that year." [5]

In a privately printed—beautifully printed it is—autobiography entitled *Dakota Days* by Edson C. Dayton, who after ranching in North Dakota during the eighties and nineties returned to his gracious homeland in western New York, I find estimates of Milton's poetry and Gladstone's character. Dayton speaks of the "intellectual face" of a certain Dakota man. Watching the features of his young range manager "aglow with pride" in a pair of buggy horses behind which they were riding, he remembered these lines from a college classmate's poem:

[5] Esther Felt Bentley, "A Conversation with Mr. Rollins," *The Princeton University Library Chronicle,* IX, No. 4 (June, 1948), 189.

*I have some kinship with the bee,*
*I am boon brother with the tree;*
*The breathing earth is part of me.*

No such quality of intellect and spirit is expressed in the auto-biographic literature of the range South of 36.

It is moralistic reading, insofar as reading of any kind is re-called, that cowboy chroniclers of the Southwest record. One day in 1885 while Frank S. Gray and his mother were sitting on the front porch of their ranch home in San Saba County, Texas, "an old man drove up in a buggy. He hitched his horse to the rack and came in carrying a heavy box and unpacked a fine assortment of Bibles. He had prayer books, hymns, psalms, concordances and Bible dictionaries, most of them bound in flexible morocco and illustrated. It was about noon, and Mother asked the old man to take out his horse and feed him while she pre-pared dinner. When I brought in the wood for the kitchen fire, she said, 'Frank, I would be pleased if you would get some of those religious books.' Since I was rambling around, she said she would not ask me to read the entire Bible but to buy the four gospels, Matthew, Mark, Luke and John, and study them.

"After the old peddler had returned thanks at the table, he told us that he was a superannuated minister of the gospel now saving lost sheep by providing them with Christian literature. When we finished our meal, I, more to gratify my mother's wish than my own desire, bought the four little gospels in flexible leather. I took them back with me to Edwards County [where my brothers and I had started a ranch] and there read them. As my mother had said, they gave me a correct idea of the Christian religion. The other boys in the monotonous bachelors' cow camp, not having anything else to read, read them also." [6]

[6] Frank S. Gray, *Pioneering in Southwest Texas* (Austin, Texas, 1949), pp. 145-46.

The autobiographic literature of the range may be classified into two categories: civilized and uncivilized, though there are shadings of both. I have gone through a long list of titles and picked out twelve that reflect cultivated minds and civilized perspective. They are: *My Life on the Range,* by John Clay; *Cattle, Horses and Men,* by John Culley; *Some Recollections of a Western Ranchman,* by William French; *A Ranchman's Recollections,* by Frank S. Hastings; *The Great Western Trail,* by Clinton Parks Lampman; *Ranching with Roosevelt,* by Lincoln A. Lang; *Cow Range and Hunting Trail,* by Malcolm S. Mackay; *Ranch Life and the Hunting Trail,* by Theodore Roosevelt; *Bucking the Sagebrush,* by Charles J. Stedman; *Forty Years on the Frontier,* by Granville Stuart; *A Tenderfoot in Colorado,* along with *The Tenderfoot in New Mexico,* both of them by R. B. Townshend.

The eleven writers of these books were all landowners as well as men of education. Not one of them was native to the range or a hired hand, as was Siringo. Hastings, the only Texan—by adoption—in the group, managed a big plains outfit that was owned in New York. Four of the writers were British. The vast coast and brush ranges of Texas that during a swift quarter of a century sent millions of Longhorn cattle north clear to the Plains of Alberta, and with them a few thousand cowboys who stamped their type upon the whole Western cow country, are not represented by a single autobiographer that can be called civilized.

The varied recollections assembled by George W. Saunders into two volumes called *The Trail Drivers of Texas* and the separately published recollections of Jack Potter, Frank Millard, Bob Lauderdale, Charlie Siringo and other men of the original cow country of Texas are rawhide in nature. They are bedrock history. They tell much, but because of a lack of that perspective which gives the writer a sense of values, they often miss much.

Curious as to what congeniality towards book-writing the rol-

licky young "stove-up cowpuncher" might have found in Caldwell, Kansas, where he was writing the story of his life in 1884,
and as to what impression his book when published might have
made on his neighbors, I ran through the files of Caldwell newspapers (weeklies) preserved in the excellent library of the
Kansas State Historical Society at Topeka.

As a "merchant" in Caldwell from the fall of 1883 to the
spring of 1886, Siringo believed in advertising as well as in himself. "Charlie Siringo," one of the paid-for local items went,
"wants every cowpuncher, nester and Chinaman in the United
States to know that he makes a specialty of fine cigars and tobacco." On June 5, 1884, the *Caldwell Standard* notified the
public that "Charlie Siringo has opened his ice cream parlor and
is now prepared to serve ice cream and cake, lemonade, and con-
fectionaries and fruits of all kinds at almost any hour of the day
or night." The *Caldwell Journal* of February 19, 1885, advertises
Siringo and Pruyne's "Oyster Parlor, where you can get a good
lunch, with a hot cup of coffee—none of your weak jim-crow
stuff, but genuine cowpuncher coffee that will almost stand alone
—thrown in."

There was a book store in town, selling things besides books.
Among articles on the cattle drives, "Texas fever," wire cutting,
killings, rattlesnake cures and many other frontier subjects, the
Caldwell papers occasionally printed discussions of books,
Thackeray's novels and Carlyle's *Frederick the Great* among
others. An account of Joseph E. Badger, Jr. living at Frankfort,
Kansas, probably interested Siringo particularly. Joseph E.
Badger, Jr. was writing five-and-ten-cent novels for Beadle, get-
ting $100 for a five-cent novel and $200 for a ten-cent novel. It
took him two weeks to write a novel, though Colonel Prentiss
Ingraham could turn out one in twenty-four hours.

The editor of the *Caldwell Journal* evidently believed that the
reading public was interested in cowboys, for he reprinted from

New York and Chicago papers articles about "The Real Cow Boy" and a satire on cowboy singing to cattle. Immediately after word come that Henry Brown, marshall of Caldwell, had been killed at Medicine Lodge, Kansas, while attempting to rob a bank, the *Standard* issued an extra, May 8, 1884. Brown had for a time been a member of Billy the Kid's gang. The *Standard* secured a statement from Charlie Siringo detailing Brown's career. Siringo carried the dossiers of a thousand men in his mind. The *Standard* also published a "Sketch of Billy the Kid's Life," written by "one of the most respectable men in Sumner County, who led a party to assist in the capture of the Kid and who was on his trail when Pat Garrett killed him." This "respectable" citizen could have been none other than Siringo. The sketch, about three hundred words in length and very succinct, was probably the first piece of his writing to get into print. I don't know just when Siringo began writing *A Texas Cowboy*—with Billy the Kid in it—but it could hardly have been later than 1884.

On September 17 and again on September 24, 1885, the *Journal* printed in large type this notice: "New Book. A Texas Cow-Boy, or Fifteen Years on the Hurricane Deck of a Spanish Pony. Watch for its announcement shortly." On October 8 the announcement came. Charles A. Siringo, according to it, "has drifted over the ranges of Texas, Indian Territory, Kansas, New Mexico and parts of Old Mexico ever since the spring of 1867. The book is now in press and will be sold only by subscription. Order early, as there are only a limited number of copies in the forthcoming edition. Price $1.00. Address the publishers, M. Umbdenstock & Co., 134 Madison Street, Chicago, Illinois. For an agency, write to the author at Caldwell, Kansas."

On December 24, 1885, the *Journal* printed a one-paragraph review, as follows:

"The latest book that has come to our table is Chas. A. Siringo's 'Texas Cowboy.' The story is that of a boy without a home, thrown upon his own resources to rustle a living out of the world. Mr. Siringo's style of narrative is better than one would expect from the chances he has had. He writes easily, and in language that all can understand. We, in reviewing the book, have learned many new things concerning the way the cattle business was conducted in the early days of that industry in the Southwest. It appears that the 'Mavricking' business after the close of the war was about the leading industry; and all it took then to make a cattle king of one's self was gall and a good branding iron. Having worked for most of the early cattle kings and drovers of Southern Texas, Mr. Siringo in very plain language shows up the methods of increasing herds that were in vogue in those days. If the book had been condensed one fourth it would have given more general satisfaction to those who wish to learn of the early days of the cattle industry; but to the great reading public it will give far better satisfaction than the works of young authors usually do."

The *Journal* was a little pink, as would be said these days, on the subject of "cattle kings." There were many more sod-house nesters in the country—and the kings of finance had not yet taken over the country's newspapers, even country weeklies. It was not nearly so pink as the *Oklahoma War Chief,* which stood militantly for "homes for the homeless and land for the landless," especially land in the Cherokee Strip, and which boiled with antipathy against "cattle barons" and preached the philosophy of Henry George. As a civic booster, Siringo helped move the Oklahoma Boomers and their *War Chief* to Caldwell about the time he was leaving for Chicago—and the Pinkertons.

Pinkerton's National Detective Agency was both rain and drouth to Siringo as a writer. For twenty-two years he was a detective in the pay of the Agency and, in his own words, was during all that time gathering "material for a second volume." By

1910 he had written the book on his experiences as a detective. From then until the end of his life the Agency blocked him and kept the "tiger blood" in him boiling. For two years publication of his *Pinkerton's Cowboy Detective* was held up in the Superior Court of Chicago—until he changed the title to *A Cowboy Detective,* changed the name of Pinkerton's National Detective Agency to Dickenson Detective Agency, substituted other fictitious names, and cut out a good deal of material. The Agency's protests were "undoubtedly rightful," Siringo's hand wrote in the preface to *A Cowboy Detective* as published.

Conscience—long delayed—and "tiger blood" did not say so, however. Three years later Siringo published in Chicago, under the nose of Pinkerton's National Detective Agency headquarters, exactly what he felt concerning "the most corrupt institution of the century." The Agency probably surmised that to take public action against *Two Evil Isms: Pinkertonism and Anarchism* would spread its views; the Agency did nothing, and the slight book seems to have done nothing.

More than anything else that Siringo wrote, however, this book reveals the workings of his matured mind towards society. In the beginning, his sympathies were with labor, and it was only when he saw anarchists betraying labor that he sought a job with Pinkerton's to bring them to justice. Very soon his eyes were opened. The falsities in reports about anarchists made by Agency men "would make a decent man's blood boil." Perjured testimony, "third degree" brutality and padded expense accounts were other Agency evils that he felt—after long delay —called upon to expose. In *A Cowboy Detective* he called Tom Horn, of the Johnson County War fame, in Wyoming, "Tim Corn" and said that he was working for "private parties." In *Two Evil Isms* he boldly says that Horn was hired by the Agency to help "wealthy cattlemen get rid of small ranchmen" at six hundred dollars a head. The latest biography of Tom Horn corroborates the statement. Siringo's years of sleuthing left "one dark blot" on his conscience. That was his work against coal miners in their fight to wring justice from "greedy corporations." Not all the books concerning the Haymarket Riots, which initiated Siringo into his detective career, have yet been written; *Two Evil Isms* is a pointed source on the subject.

For years before *Riata and Spurs* appeared, in 1927, the dogs appeared to be sleeping. Now, vengeance in their voices, they opened up on Siringo again. Of the twenty chapters in his new book, eleven had been transposed, with revisions, from *A Cowboy Detective*. Actual names now took the place of the fictions that had been imposed by the Pinkertons. Among these actual names was that of Pinkerton's National Detective Agency, mentioned without criticism. There was nothing actionable in Siringo's use of their name, but the Pinkertons objected to his printing it. They bluffed the publishers into causing him to cut out about 150 pages relating his experiences as a detective and to substitute therefor material meant for another book to be entitled *Bad Men of the West*. This wholesale deletion and substitution made the second and subsequent printings of *Riata and Spurs* a very different book from the first, though no word of explanation in the second printing so indicates.

I never saw Charlie Siringo. I was not interested in him until about four years before his death. Really, I am not so much interested in him now as I was then. A matured sense of values tells me that it is much more important for more people to read *The Trial and Death of Socrates* than it is that anybody read *Fifteen Years on the Hurricane Deck of a Spanish Pony*. However that may be, some details that Siringo left out of his self-portraits belong here.

Remembering him out of the days of the bloody Coeur d'Alene strike in Idaho, 1891-92, John Hays Hammond described him as "a slender, wiry man, dark-eyed, dark-moustached, modest. Lately recovered of smallpox, he was noticeably pitted. This would be an undisguisable identification in a tight place, but he did not seem to mind. . . . He was the most interesting, resourceful, courageous detective I ever dealt with."[7]

A lawyer who worked with Siringo in "the Mining War" and who wrote a book of reminiscences in which Siringo is the chief figure, thus describes him: "He was deadly with a Colt's 45, a weapon he carried at all times. I have thrown up an empty bean can and watched him, shooting from the hip, riddle it in flight; yet he had never, so far as anyone knows, taken a human life. . . . He was shrewdly intelligent, infallible in his judgment of human nature, and courageous to the point of recklessness; he was quick and nervous normally, but in a critical moment, or an emergency, cold and steady as a rock. He was relentless on a scent. He was a rattler who never struck—a personality as interesting as any I have met along the frontier."[8]

Just before old Charlie was about to mount the pale horse and ride away into the dark, two writers of the West pictured him in such a way that the main features of their portraits might be undated. "A small man, weighing barely a hundred and thirty pounds, but wire-tough, brown of face, and keen of eye, with humor still invincible in spite of his seventy-two years," wrote Neil M. Clark.[9]

[7] John Hays Hammond, "Strong Men of the West," *Scribner's Magazine,* February and March, 1925. In *The Autobiography of John Hays Hammond* (New York, 1925, I, 191-96) Hammond details the work of Siringo in the strikes, but does not describe him so specifically.

[8] William A. Stoll, *Silver Strike* (Boston, 1932), p. 183.

[9] Neil M. Clark, "Close Calls: An Interview with Charles A. Siringo," *The American Magazine,* January, 1929. In this interview Neil Clark makes an intelligent interpretation of Siringo's philosophy on bad men—something missing in two articles purporting to be from "Letters of Charley Siringo," by Raymond D. Thorp, in *Western Sportsman,* Denver, Colorado, July and August, 1940.

The next picture is from Siringo's old friend Gene Rhodes, the gallant. "Faded brown eyes, but sharp eyes that never miss the slightest movement of any person or anything. Not nervous, but always alert. A thin face, brown like saddle leather; wind and sun have tanned that face beyond all changing. Most expressive hands; thumbs especially; thumbs which fill out and picture forth the story as he talks; a trigger finger that sticks out with every gesture. Fascinating forefinger. You can't take your eyes from it. Thin lipped; a mouth that would be hard if it were not for an occasional quirk of humor. Quite a frank smile, and often a chuckle. Not a tall man; slender—yes, frail. You note this with a shock; listening, not once had you thought of him as a small man or as an old one. A small head, a boy's head. And he is a boy, full of mischief and keen fun. Looks right at you when you talk, but always notices what anyone else happens to be doing. . . . Small feet. Corded throat. . . . Carries a loaded cane; polished steer-horn tips on a steel rod; probably made for him in a penitentiary. Wears a small red silk handkerchief, a low-crowned Stetson, neat clothing and shoes; not boots. Straight back; does not stoop; head carried like Chanticleer." [10]

Charlie Siringo had almost nothing to say on life; he reported actions. He put down something valid on a class of livers, as remote now from the Atomic Age as Rameses II. His cowboys and gunmen were not of Hollywood and folklore. He was an honest reporter.

[10] Eugene M. Rhodes, "He'll Make a Hand," *Sunset Magazine,* June, 1927.

# BIBLIOGRAPHY OF SIRINGO'S WRITINGS

1) *A Texas Cow Boy or, Fifteen Years on the Hurricane Deck of a Spanish Pony*. Taken from Real Life by Chas. A. Siringo, An Old Stove Up "Cow Puncher," Who Has Spent Nearly Twenty Years on the Great Western Cattle Ranges. Chicago: M. Umbdenstock & Co., Publishers, 1885. Pp. xii + 316. Cloth.

The 1886 edition has identical title page except for the name of Siringo & Dobson, Publishers, Chicago. Pp. xii + 316 + Addenda (pp. 317-47). Cloth.

1893 edition. Title page has been reset without change of wording, except for name of publisher: The Eagle Publishing Co., Chicago, 1893. Pp. 347 + 4 pp. advertising of books published by Eagle Publishing Company and Rand, McNally & Co. Cloth. This 1893 printing seems not to have been the third. An undated printing, paper-bound, using both colored frontispieces of the first edition and showing typographical evidence of having been made prior to the 1893 printing, bears the imprint of Rand, McNally & Co., 148 to 154 Monroe Street, Chicago, and 323 Broadway, New York. The type seems less worn. The Eagle Publishing Co., the name of which is in the 1893 edition, seems to have been a subsidiary of Rand, McNally & Co.

Probably not long after 1893, Rand, McNally and Company issued the book as No. 56 in their Globe Library series. The title page, undated, is reset. Pp. 347 + several pages of railroad advertisements at front and back. Paper back. Variations in weight of paper on which the book is printed occur over the years during which Rand, McNally kept the book in print—until 1912.

For the final form of printing, 1914-1926, the book was entirely reset, in smaller font type, and run off on cheaper pulp paper than that used by Rand, McNally. Title page, undated, is under imprint of the J. S. Ogilvie Publishing Company, 57 Rose Street, New York. Pp. 251, including a 6-page "Publisher's Note," + 5 or 6 pp. of book advertisements that changed from year to year.

2) *A Cowboy Detective*. A True Story of Twenty-Two Years with a World-Famous Detective Agency. Giving Inside Facts of the Bloody Coeur d'Alene Labor Riots, and the Many Ups and Downs of the Author throughout the United States, Alaska, British Columbia and Old Mexico. Also Exciting Scenes among the Moonshiners of Kentucky and Virginia. By Chas. A. Siringo, Author of "A Texas Cowboy." Chicago: W. B. Conkey Company, 1912. Copyright 1912 by Chas. A. Siringo. Pp. 519. Cloth.

In October, 1921, as I know by a letter from the publishers, the J. S. Ogilvie Publishing Company, 57 Rose Street, New York, issued *A Cowboy Detective* in two volumes, the first under that title, pp. 246 + advertisements, and the second under the title of *Further Adventures of a Cowboy Detective*, pp. 247-519 + advertisements. The two paper-bound books made Nos. 127 and 128 in the Railroad Series. They sold at twenty-five cents each. None were printed after 1924.

3) *Two Evil Isms: Pinkertonism and Anarchism*. By a Cowboy Detective Who Knows, as He Spent Twenty-Two Years in the Inner Circle of Pinkerton's National Detective Agency. By Charles A. Siringo, Author of "A Texas Cowboy" and "A Cowboy Detective." Price 25 cents. Charles A. Siringo, Publisher. P.O. Box 396, Chicago, Ill. Copyright 1915 by Chas. A. Siringo. All rights reserved. Pp. 110. Paper covers.

4) *A Lone Star Cowboy*. Being fifty years experience in the saddle as Cowboy, Detective and New Mexico Ranger, on every cow trail in the wooly old west. Also the doings of some "bad" cowboys, such as "Billy the Kid," Wess Harding and "Kid Curry." By Chas. A. Siringo, Author of "Fifteen Years on the Hurricane Deck of a Spanish Pony" and "A Cowboy Detective." Santa Fe, New Mexico, 1919. Pp. 290. Cloth.

Reverse side of the title page bears copyright date of 1919. Publisher of book is not given, but it was Siringo. Preceding title page is a page advertising *A Song Companion of A Lone Star Cowboy,* with the author's address: Box 322, Santa Fe, New Mexico. A second printing, or perhaps only a second binding, of the book adds one page plus advertisements of Siringo's *History of Billy the Kid* as well as of *A Cowboy Detective* and *A Song Companion*. This second form of the book also contains, unpaged, List of Illustrations and Contents.

5) *A Song Companion of A Lone Star Cowboy*. Old Favorite Cow-Camp Songs. Price 35 cents. By Chas. A. Siringo, of Santa Fe, New Mexico, Author of "A Lone Star Cowboy" and "A Cowboy Detective." Copyright 1919. Pp. 42. Paper covers. (A shoddy collection.)

6) *History of "Billy the Kid."* The true life of the most daring young outlaw of the age. . . . By Chas. A. Siringo. Santa Fe, New Mexico, 1920. Copyright 1920. Pp. 142. Paper covers. No publisher named, but the book was issued by Siringo. At back a page advertises three other books of his and gives his Santa Fe address.

7) *Riata and Spurs*. The Story of a Lifetime spent in the Saddle as Cowboy and Detective. By Charles A. Siringo. With an Introduction by Gifford Pinchot. And with Illustrations. Bos-

ton and New York: Houghton Mifflin Company, The Riverside Press, Cambridge, 1927. Pp. xiv + 276. Cloth.

After the first printing, pages 120-268 of *Riata and Spurs* were suppressed. Substitute material was printed, bringing the total number of pages up to 261. No notice in the revised edition informs the reader that more than half of the book is composed of material entirely different from that contained in the first edition. Matter pertaining to Siringo's experiences as a Pinkerton detective was cut out and accounts of bad men were substituted.

# A TEXAS COW BOY

OR,

## FIFTEEN YEARS

ON THE

## Hurricane Deck of a Spanish Pony.

TAKEN FROM REAL LIFE

BY

## CHAS. A. SIRINGO,

AN OLD STOVE UP "COW PUNCHER," WHO HAS SPENT
NEARLY TWENTY YEARS ON THE GREAT
WESTERN CATTLE RANGES.

---

M. UMBDENSTOCK & CO., Publishers,
CHICAGO, ILLINOIS.
1885.

*Title page of first edition*

THE AUTHOR,
IN COW BOY UNIFORM.

*Fly sheet of first edition*

# AUTHOR'S PREFACE

$M$Y EXCUSE for writing this book is money—and lots of it. ✓

I suppose the above would suffice, but as time is not very precious I will continue and tell how the idea of writing a book first got into my head:

While ranching on the Indian Territory line, close to Caldwell, Kansas, in the winter of '82 and '83, we boys—there being nine of us—made an iron-clad rule that whoever was heard swearing or caught picking grey backs off and throwing them on the floor without first killing them, should pay a fine of ten cents for each and every offense. The proceeds to be used for buying choice literature—something that would have a tendency to raise us above the average cow-puncher. Just twenty-four hours after making this rule we had three dollars in the pot—or at least in my pocket, I having been appointed treasurer.

As I was going to town that night to see my Sunday girl, I proposed to the boys that, while up there, I send the money off for a years subscription to some good newspaper. The question then came up, what paper shall it be? We finally agreed to leave it to a vote—each man to write the one of his choice on a slip of paper and drop it in a hat. There being two young Texans present who could neither read nor write, we let them *speak* their choice after the rest of us got our votes deposited. At the word given them to cut loose they both yelled "Police Gazette," and on asking why they voted for that wicked Sheet, they both replied as though with one voice: "Cause we can read the pictures." We found, on counting the votes that the Police Gazette had won, so it was subscribed for.

3

With the first copy that arrived was the beginning of a continued story, entitled "Potts turning Paris inside out." Mr. Potts, the hero, was an old stove-up New York preacher, who had made a raise of several hundred thousand dollars and was over in Paris blowing it in. I became interested in the story, and envied Mr. Potts very much. I wished for a few hundred thousand so I could do likewise; I lay awake one whole night trying to study up a plan by which I could make the desired amount. But, thinks I, what can an uneducated cow puncher do now-a-days to make such a vast sum? In trying to solve the question my mind darted back a few years, when, if I had taken time by the forelock, I might have now been wallowing in wealth with the rest of the big cattle kings—or to use a more appropriate name, cattle thieves. But alas! thought I, the days of honorable cattle stealing is past, and I must turn my mind into a healthier channel.

The next morning while awaiting breakfast I happened to pick up a small scrap of paper and read: "To the young man of high aims literature offers big inducements, providing he gets into an untrodden field."

That night I lay awake again, trying to locate some "cussed" untrodden field, where, as an author, I might soar on high—to the extent of a few hundred thousand at least.

At last, just as our pet rooster, "Deacon Bates" was crowing for day, I found a field that I had never heard of any one trampling over—a "nigger" love story. So that night I launched out on my new novel, the title of which was, "A pair of two-legged coons." My heroine, Miss Patsy Washington was one shade darker than the ace of spades, while her lover, Mr. Andrew Jackson, was three colors darker than herself. My plot was laid in African Bend on the Colorado river in Southern Texas.

Everything went on nicely, until about half way through the first chapter, when Mr. Jackson was convicted and sent to Hunts-

4

ville for stealing a neighbors hog; and while I was trying to find a substitute for him, old Patsy flew the track and eloped with a Yankee carpet-bagger. That was more than I could endure, so picking up the manuscript I threw it into the fire. Thus ended my first attempt at Authorship.

I then began figuring up an easier field for my inexperienced pen, and finally hit upon the idea of writing a history of my own short, but rugged life, which dear reader you have before you. But whether it will bring me in "shekels" enough to capsize Paris remains yet to be "disskivered" as the Negro says.

# 1. MY BOYHOOD DAYS

I T WAS a bright morning, on the 7th day of February 1856, as near as I can remember, that your humble Servant came prancing into this wide and wicked world.

By glancing over the map you will find his birth-place, at the extreme southern part of the Lone Star State, on the Peninsula of Matagorda, a narrow strip of land bordered by the Gulf of Mexico on the south and Matagorda Bay on the north.

This Peninsula is from one to two miles wide and seventy five miles long. It connects the mainland at Caney and comes to a focus at Deskrows Point or "Salura Pass." About midway between the two was situated the "Dutch Settlement," and in the centre of that Settlement, which contained only a dozen houses, stood the little frame cottage that first gave me shelter.

My father who died when I was only a year old, came from the sunny clime of Italy, while my dear old mother drifted from the Boggs of good "ould" Ireland. Am I not a queer conglomerate—a sweet-scented mixture indeed!

Our nearest neighbor was a kind old soul by the name of John Williams, whose family consisted of his wife and eleven children.

7

In the fall of 1859 I took my first lessons in school, my teacher being a Mr. Hale from Illinois.

The school house, a little old frame building, stood off by itself, about a mile from the Settlement, and we little tow-heads, sister and I, had to hoof it up there every morning, through the grassburrs, barefooted; our little sunbrowned feet had never been incased in shoe-leather up to that time.

To avoid the grassburrs, sometimes on getting an early start we would go around by the Gulf beach which was quite a distance out of our way. In taking this route though, I would generally be late at school, for there were so many little things to detain me—such as trying to catch the shadow of a flying sea gull, or trying to lasso sand crabs on my stick horse.

Crowds of Cow Boys used to come over to the Peninsula from the mainland and sometimes have occasion to rope wild steers in my presence—hence me trying to imitate them.

I remember getting into a scrape once by taking the beach route to school; sister who was a year older than I, was walking along the water edge picking up pretty shells while I was riding along on my stick horse taking the kinks out of my rope—a piece of fishline—so as to be ready to take in the first crab that showed himself. Those crabs went in large droves and sometimes ventured quite a distance out from the Gulf, but on seeing a person would break for the water.

It was not long before I spied a large drove on ahead, pulling their freight for the water. I put spurs to my pony and dashed after them. I managed to get one old fat fellow headed off and turned towards the prairie. I threw at him several times but he would always go through the loop before I could pull it up. He finally struck a hole and disappeared.

I was determined to get him out and take another whirl at him, so dropping my horse and getting down on all fours I began digging the sand away with my hands, dog fashion.

About that time sister came up and told me to come on as I would be late at school, etc.

I think I told her to please go to Halifax, as I was going to rope that crab before I quit or "bust." At any rate she went off, leaving me digging with all my might.

Every now and then I would play dog by sticking my snoot down in the hole to smell. But I rammed it down once too often. Mr. Crab was nearer the surface than I thought for. He was laying for me. I gave a comanche yell, jumped ten feet in the air and lit out for home at a 2:40 gait. One of his claws was fastened to my upper lip while the other clamped my nose with an iron-like grip.

I met Mr. William Berge coming out to the beach after a load of wood, and he relieved me of my uncomfortable burden. He had to break the crabs claws off to get him loose.

I arrived at school just as Mr. Hale was ringing the bell after recess. He called me up and wanted to know what was the matter with my face, it was so bloody. Being a little George W., minus the hatchet, I told him the truth. Suffice to say he laid me across his knee and made me think a nest of bumble bees were having a dance in the seat of my breeches—or at least where the seat should have been. I never had a pair of pants on up to that time. Had worn nothing but a long white shirt made of a flour sack after some of the "big bugs" in Matagorda had eaten the flour out.

The fall of 1861 Mr. Hale broke up school and left for Yankeedom to join the blue coats. And from that time on I had a regular picnic, doing nothing and studying mischief. Billy Williams was my particular chum; we were constantly together doing some kind of devilment. The old women used to say we were the meanest little imps in the Settlement, and that we would be hung before we were twenty-one. Our three favorite passtimes were, riding the milk calves, coon hunting and sailing playboats down on the bay shore.

9

Shortly after school broke up I wore my first pair of breeches. Uncle "Nick" and aunt "Mary," mothers' brother and sister, who lived in Galveston, sent us a trunk full of clothes and among them was a pair of white canvas breeches for me.

The first Sunday after the goods arrived mother made me scour myself all over and try my new pants on. They were large enough for two kids of my size, but mother said I could wear them that day if I would be a good boy, and that she would take a few tucks in them before the next Sunday. So after getting me fixed up she told me not to leave the yard or she would skin me alive, etc.

Of course I should have been proud of the new addition to my wardrobe and like a good little boy obeyed my mother; but I wasn't a good little boy and besides the glory of wearing white pants was insignificant compared to that of an exciting coon hunt with dogs through brush, bramble and rushes. You see I had promised Billy the evening before to go coon hunting with him that day.

I watched my chance and while mother was dressing sister in her new frock I tiptoed out of the house and skipped.

Billy was waiting for me with the four dogs and off we went for the Bay shore.

Arriving there the dogs disappeared in the tall rushes barking at every jump; we jumped right in after them, up to our waists in the mud. We had a genuine good all-day coon hunt, killing several coons and one wild cat.

We gave up the hunt about sundown, and I started for home, the glory of my new pants having departed. I was indeed a sorry looking sight, covered with mud from head to foot.

I entered the house with some fear and trembling, and well I might, for mother was "laying" for me with the old black strap. The result was I slept sound that night, but couldn't sit down without pain for a week afterwards.

## 2. MY INTRODUCTION TO THE LATE WAR

I T WAS Monday morning—a day that I despised. Need you wonder, for it was mother's wash day and I had to carry wood from the Gulf beach to keep the "pot boiling."

I tried to play off sick that morning but it would not work, for mother had noticed that I got away with two plates of mush besides three hard boiled eggs for breakfast.

Before starting out after my first load of wood, I hid the big old strap which hung by the door, for I felt it in my bones there was war in the air. I always did have a tough time of it on wash days, and I knew this Monday would bring the same old story.

At last mother got the fire started under the wash-pot which stood out in the yard and told me for about the twentieth time to go after an armful of wood. I hesitated, in hopes that she would take a notion to go herself, but when she stamped her foot and picked up a barrel stave I knew I had better be going, for when she got her Irish blood up it was dangerous to linger.

When I got out among the drift wood on the beach, I treed a cotton-tail rabbit up a hollow log, and I made up my mind to get Mr. cotton-tail out, wood or no wood.

I began digging the sand away from the log as fast as I could so as to be able to roll it down into the Gulf and drown the rabbit out.

It was a very hot day and digging the heavy sand with only my hands and a stick was slow, tiresome work. The result was I fell asleep with my head under the log and my bare legs sticking out in the hot June sun. I dreamt I died and went to a dreadful hot country and Satan was there piling hot coals on me.

Finally the sun went under a cloud, or at least I suppose it did, for the burning pain left me and I began to dream of Heaven; I thought the Lord was there sitting upon His throne of gold in the midst of scores of happy children. Calling me up to him he pointed to a large pile of fence rails down in a beautiful valley and said: "my boy you go down and carry every one of those rails up here to me before you stop."

His words landed up against my happy thoughts like a thunderbolt from a clear sky. I had been thinking of what a picnic I would have with the other children.

A walk of about one mile brought me to the pile of rails; there were more in the pile than I could count, I shouldered one of the lightest and struck out up the steep hill, thinking how I would like to be back with mother, even if I had to carry an armful of wood from the beach now and then.

When about half way up the hill I heard a terrible noise such as I had never heard before, it awakened me, and in trying to jump up I bumped my head against the log, and also filled my eyes full of sand.

When I got onto my feet and the sand out of my eyes, I discovered the whole beach, east of me, thronged with men carrying guns, and marching right towards me. The head ones were not over a hundred yards off, beating drums and blowing their horns.

It is needless to say I was scared and that I ran as fast as my legs could carry me, looking back every minute to see if they were after me. It was in this way that I ran or sprang right into the midst of Mrs. Zipprian's drove of geese, before I knew it. There were several old ganders in the drove which used to chase me every chance they got. I generally took particular pains to go around them; but this time my mind was in a different channel from what it had ever been in before, hence my not looking out for them.

As I flew past, two of the old ganders made a dive at me, but only one succeeded in catching on; he grabbed the tail of my shirt, which stuck straight out behind, in his mouth and hung on with blood in his eyes. My speed seemed to increase instead of slacken, every time the old gander would bounce up and come down, his claws would rake the skin from the calves of my legs. His death-like grip finally broke loose and I felt considerable lighter. My mind also, felt somewhat relieved.

Mother was out in the yard washing, she had picked up chips enough to boil the water; the tub was sitting upon a box and she was rubbing away with all her might, her back towards me. As I was looking over my shoulder I ran against her, knocking her, tub and all over in a pile, myself with them.

Mother got up first with her right hand in my shirt collar, I plead manfully and tried to tell her about the scores of men, but she was too mad to listen, she dragged me to where the big black strap should have hung, I knew she couldn't find it, therefore hoped to get off with a few slaps, but alas, no, she spied the mush stick and the way she gave it to me with that was a caution!

The crowd I saw proved to be Dr. Pierceson's company of rebels, who had been sent over from Matagorda to drill and be ready to fight the bluecoats when they came. It was then the summer of 1862. They located their camp on the beach, about a mile from our house, and I used to march with them all day long sometimes. The captain, Dr. Pierceson, gave me an umbrella stick which I used for a gun.                    13

That coming fall about five thousand Yankees landed at Deckrows Point on the Peninsula and marched by our ranch on their way to the rebel camp which was stationed forty miles above, at the mouth of Caney Creek.

They camped one night close to our house and filled me up with hard-tack, which was quite a treat to a fellow living on mush and milk.

They had a five or six day fight with the rebels, neither of them coming off victorious. We could hear the guns plainly from the "Settlement." Many dead men were washed ashore on the beach. My sister and I stumbled onto one poor fellow one day, shot through the heart. His clothes were gone and his wrist was marked "J. T." in India ink.

After the battle the Yankees marched back to Deckrows Point where they remained to the end of the war; the rebels still held their ground at the mouth of Caney. Every now and then a squad from each side would meet at the "Settlement" and have a skirmish. I remember once after one of those skirmishes a crowd of Yankees rounded Mr. Williams up on the prairie—Billy and I being with him—and throwing their pistols in his face told him if they ever found him so far from home again they would kill him.

Their threats didn't scare Mr. Williams the least bit, for he afterwards slipped into their camp after dark and stole eleven head of their best horses and gave them to the rebels. But on his way back from the rebel camp, where he went to take the horses they caught him and took him aboard of a Yankee man-of-war to hang him. They had the rope around his neck ready to swing him when the General turned him loose, on account of his old age and bravery, telling him never to be caught from home again.

Fighting was going on nearly every day in sight of us; sometimes the Yankee gun boats would get into the Bay among the rebel boats, and at other times they would fight across the narrow strip of land, shooting right over the houses at one another. Many of the cannon balls dropped on the prairie; one of them at one time struck within a few feet of Mr. Williams, almost burying him in the sand as it plowed along on the ground. Poor fellow, he was afterwards killed by one, he carried one home and taking all the powder out of it, as he supposed, set it out in the yard with the hole up, and then told Billy to get him a coal of fire in the tongs. He thought it would just flash a little.

I was present, and not liking the looks of it, crept out behind the picket gate, a few yards away, and peeped between the pickets.

The whole family was looking on to see the fun, Mattie, one of the little girls, was sitting with her arms around a dog's neck, within a few feet of it.

Billy, arriving with the coal, handed it to his father who reached over and let it drop down into the hole—where he had taken out the lead screw.

It seemed to me that the coal hadn't reached the hole when the thing exploded. For a few seconds everything was enveloped in smoke; when the smoke disappeared sufficiently for me to see, the whole sky seemed to be a blaze of fire, and finally Mr. Williams emerged out of the heavy cloud of smoke hopping on one leg.

A piece of the bomb-shell had taken off part of one foot on the left leg and another piece had plowed through the calf of his right leg; part of one ear was also gone. He only lived a few days.

A piece of the shell took off one of the dog's legs without even touching Mattie, the little girl who had her arms around his neck.

Several pieces went through the house, and one piece went through the picket gate right over my head. The next day Billy and I found a large piece sticking in the wall of an old vacant house a mile from where it exploded.

During the war several ships were driven ashore on the beach by the Yankee gun boats. The folks at the "Settlement" would get all the plunder. One ship was loaded with dry goods and from that time on I wore breeches.

About a year after the war broke out the rebels gathered up all the cattle on the Peninsula and drove them to the mainland, where they were turned loose with the thousands upon thousands of wild cattle already over there. Their idea in doing so was to keep the Yankees—whom they knew would hold the lower part of the Peninsula, they having the best gunboats—from getting fresh beef to eat. There was only one cow left in the whole "Settlement" and that was our old "Browny;" mother had begged manfully for them to leave her, for she knew we children would starve to death living on mush straight.

When the war broke up everybody was happy. We cheered for joy when Mr. Joe Yeamans brought the good news from town.

Shortly after this all of the men and boys that were large enough, went over to the mainland to gather up the Peninsula cattle. On their arrival they found it a bigger job than they had figured on, for they were scattered over two or three hundred miles of country and as wild as deer.

Billy and I thought it very hard that we could not go and be Cow Boys too; but we had lots of fun all by ourselves, for we had an old mule and two or three ponies to ride, so you see we practiced riding in anticipation of the near future, when we would be large enough to be Cow Boys.

After being gone about three months the crowd came back, bringing with them several hundred head of cattle, which they had succeeded in gathering. Among them were about twenty head belonging to mother.

16

The crowd went right back after more. This stimulated Billy and I to become a crowd of Cow Boys all by ourselves, therefore we put in most of our time lassoing and riding wild yearlings, etc. We hardly stayed at home long enough to get our meals. Mother had to get her own wood in those days, for sister had gone to school in Galveston. Of course I always had to come home at night, therefore mother would get satisfaction out of me with the black strap or mush stick, after I was snugly settled in bed, for my waywardness and trifling habits.

In the spring of 1867, a cattle man by the name of Faldien brought his family over to the Peninsula for their health and rented part of our house to live in.

After getting his wife and babies located in their new quarters, he started back home, in Matagorda, to make preparations for spring work, he having to rig up new outfits, etc. He persuaded mother to let me go with him, and learn to run cattle. When she consented I was the happiest boy in the "Settlement," for my life long wish was about to be gratified.

## 3. MY FIRST LESSON IN COW PUNCHING

THE next day after arriving in town, Mr. Faldien sent me out to his ranch, twenty miles, on Big Boggy. I rode out on the "grub" wagon with the colored cook. That night, after arriving at the ranch, there being several men already there, we went out wild boar hunting. We got back about midnight very tired and almost used up. Such a hunt was very different from the coon hunts Billy and I used to have at the "Settlement." Our dogs were badly gashed up by the boars, and it was a wonder some of us hadn't been served the same way.

In a few days Mr. Faldien came out to the ranch, bringing with him several men. After spending a few days gathering up the cow-ponies, which hadn't been used since the fall before, we started for Lake Austin—a place noted for wild cattle.

During the summer I was taken sick and had to go home. I was laid up for two months with typhoid fever. Every one thought I would die.

That fall, about October, mother married a man by the name of Carrier, who hailed from Yankeedom. He claimed that he owned a farm in Michigan, besides lots of other property.

He was very anxious to get back to his farm, so persuaded mother to sell out lock, stock and barrel and go with him.

She had hard work to find a buyer as money was very scarce, but finally she got Mr. George Burkheart, a merchant in Matagorda, to set his own price on things and take them.

The house and one hundred and seventy-five acres of land only brought one hundred and seventy-five dollars. The sixty head of cattle that we had succeeded in getting back from the mainland went at one dollar a head and all others that still remained on the mainland—thrown in for good measure.

At last everything for sale was disposed of and we got "Chris" Zipprian to take us to Indianola in his schooner. We bade farewell to the old homestead with tears in our eyes. I hated more than anything else to leave old "Browny" behind for she had been a friend in need as well as a friend indeed. Often when I would be hungry and afraid to go home for fear of mother and the mush stick, she would let me go up to her on the prairie calf fashion and get my milk. She was nearly as old as myself.

At Indianola we took the Steamship "Crescent City" for New Orleans. The first night out we ran into a large Brig and came very near going under. The folks on the Brig were nearly starved to death, having been drifting about for thirty days without a rudder. We took them in tow, after getting our ship in trim again, and landed them safely in Galveston.

There was a bar-room on our ship, and our new lord and master, Mr. Carrier, put in his spare time drinking whisky and gambling; I do not think he drew a sober breath from the time we left Indianola until we landed in New Orleans, by that time he had squandered every cent received for the homestead and cattle, so mother had to go down into her stocking and bring out the little pile of gold which she had saved up before the war for "hard times," as she used to say. With this money she now bought our tickets to Saint Louis. We took passage, I think, on the "Grand Republic." There was also a bar-room on this boat, and after wheedling mother out of the remainder of her funds, he drank whisky and gambled as before, so we landed in Saint Louis without a cent.

Mother had to pawn her feather mattress and pillows for a month's rent in an old delapidated frame building on one of the back streets. It contained only four rooms, two up stairs and two down; the lower rooms were occupied by the stingy old landlord and family; we lived in one of the upper rooms, while a Mr. Socks, whose wife was an invalid, occupied the other.

The next day after getting established in our new quarters, the "old man," as I called him, struck out to find a job; he found one at a dollar a day shoveling coal.

At first he brought home a dollar every night, then a half and finally a quarter. At last he got to coming home drunk without a nickel in his pocket. He finally came up missing; we didn't know what had become of him. Mother was sick in bed at the time from worrying. I went out several times hunting work but no one would even give me a word of encouragement, with the exception of an old Jew who said he was sorry for me.

A little circumstance happened, shortly after the "old man" pulled his trifling carcass for parts unknown, which made me a better boy and no doubt a better man than I should have been had it never happened.

Everything was white without, for it had been snowing for the past two days. It was about five o'clock in the evening and the cold piercing north wind was whistling through the unceiled walls of our room. Mother was sound asleep, while sister and I sat shivering over an old, broken stove, which was almost cold, there being no fuel in the house.

Sister began crying and wondered why the Lord let us suffer so? I answered that may be it was because we quit saying our prayers. Up to the time we left Texas mother used to make us kneel down by the bed-side and repeat the Lord's prayer every night before retiring. Since then she had, from worrying, lost all interest in Heavenly affairs.

"Let us say our prayers now, then, brother!" said sister drying the tears from her eyes.

We both knelt down against the old, rusty stove and commenced. About the time we had finished the door opened and in stepped Mr. Socks with a bundle under his arm. "Here children, is a loaf of bread and some butter and I will bring you up a bucket of coal in a few moments, for I suppose from the looks of the stove you are cold," said the good man, who had just returned from his day's work.

Was ever a prayer so quickly heard? We enjoyed the bread and butter, for we hadn't tasted food since the morning before.

The next day was a nice sunny one, and I struck out up town to try and get a job shoveling snow from the sidewalks.

The first place I tackled was a large stone front on Pine street. The kind lady of the establishment said she would give me twenty-five cents if I would do a good job cleaning the sidewalk in front of the house.

After an hour's hard work I finished, and, after paying me, the lady told me to call next day and she would give me a job shoveling coal down in the cellar, as I had done an extra good job on the sidewalk. This was encouraging and I put in the whole day shoveling snow, but never found any more twenty-five cent jobs; most I received for one whole hour's work was ten cents, and then the old fat fellow kicked like a bay steer, about the d——d snow being such an expense, etc.

From that time on I made a few dimes each day sawing wood or shoveling coal and therefore got along splendid.

I forgot to mention my first evening in Saint Louis. I was going home from the bakery when I noticed a large crowd gathered in front of a corner grocery; I went up to see what they were doing. Two of the boys had just gotten through fighting when I got there; the store-keeper and four or five other men were standing in the door looking on at the crowd of boys who were trying to cap another fight.

As I walked up, hands shoved clear to the bottom of my pockets, the store-keeper called out, pointing at me, "there's a country Jake that I'll bet can lick any two boys of his size in the crowd."

Of course all eyes were then turned onto me, which, no doubt, made me look sheepish. One of the men asked me where I was from; when I told him, the store-keeper exclaimed, "by gum, if he is from Texas I'll bet two to one that he can clean out any two boys of his size in the crowd."

One of the other men took him up and they made a sham bet of ten dollars, just to get me to fight. The two boys were then picked out; one was just about my size and the other considerably smaller. They never asked me if I would take a hand in the fight until everything was ready. Of course I hated to crawl out, for fear they might think I was a coward.

Everything being ready the store-keeper called out, "dive in boys!"

We had it up and down for quite a while, finally I got the largest one down, and was putting it to him in good shape, when the other one picked up a piece of brick-bat and began pounding me on the back of the head with it. I looked up to see what he was doing and he struck me over one eye with the bat. I jumped up and the little fellow took to his heels, but I soon overtook him and blackened both of his eyes up in good shape, before the other boy, who was coming at full tilt could get there to help him. I then chased the other boy back to the crowd. That ended the fight and I received two ginger-snaps, from the big hearted store-keeper, for my trouble. I wore the nick-name of "Tex" from that time on, during my stay in that neighbor-

22

hood; and also wore a black eye, where the little fellow struck me with the bat, for several days afterwards.

About the middle of January mother received a letter from the "old man," with ten dollars enclosed, and begging her to come right on without delay as he had a good job and was doing well, etc. He was at Lebanon, Ill., twenty-five miles from the city. The sight of ten dollars and the inducements he held out made us hope that we would meet with better luck there, so we packed up our few traps and started on the Ohio and Mississippi railroad.

On arriving in Lebanon about nine o'clock at night we found the "old man" there waiting for us.

The next morning we all struck out on foot, through the deep snow, for Moore's ranch where the "old man" had a job chopping cord wood. A tramp of seven miles brought us to the little old log cabin which was to be our future home. A few rods from our cabin stood a white frame house in which lived Mr. Moore and family.

Everything went on lovely for the first week, notwithstanding that the cold winds whistled through the cracks in our little cabin, and we had nothing to eat but corn bread, black coffee and old salt pork that Moore could not find a market for.

The first Saturday after getting established in our new home the "old man" went to town and got on a glorious drunk, squandered every nickel he could rake and scrape; from that time on his visits to town were more frequent than his trips to the woods, to work. At last I was compelled to go to work for Moore at eight dollars a month, to help keep the wolf from our door, and don't you forget it, I earned eight dollars a month, working out in the cold without gloves and only half clothed.

Towards spring the "old man" got so mean and good-for-nothing that the neighbors had to run him out of the country. A crowd of them surrounded the house one night, took the old

23

fellow out and preached him a sermon; then they gave him until morning to either skip or be hung. You bet he didn't wait until morning.

A short while afterwards mother took sister and went to town to hunt work. She left her household goods with one of the near neighbors, a Mr. Muck, where they still remain I suppose, if not worn out. But there was nothing worth hauling off except the dishes. I must say the table ware was good; we had gotten them from a Spanish vessel wrecked on the Gulf beach during the war.

Mother found work in a private boarding house, and sister with a Mrs. Bell, a miller's wife, while I still remained with Moore at the same old wages.

Along in June sometime I quit Moore on account of having the ague. I thought I should have money enough to take a rest until I got well, but bless you I only had ninety cents to my credit, Moore had deducted thirty-five dollars the "old man" owed him out of my earnings. I pulled for town as mad as an old setting hen. But I soon found work again, with an old fellow by the name of John Sargent, who was to give me eight dollars a month, board and clothes and pay my doctor bills.

About the first of September mother and sister went to Saint Louis where they thought wages would be higher. They bade me good bye, promising to find me a place in the city, so I could be with them; also promised to write.

Shortly afterwards I quit Mr. Sargent with only one dollar to my credit; and that I haven't got yet. He charged me up with everything I got in the shape of clothes, doctor bills, medicine, etc.

I then went to work for a carpenter, to learn the trade, for my board, clothes, etc. I was to remain with him three years. My first day's work was turning a big heavy stone for him to grind a lot of old, rusty tools on. That night after supper I broke my con-

24

tract, as I concluded that I knew just as much about the carpenter's trade as I wished to know, and skipped for the country, by moonlight.

I landed up at a Mr. Jacobs' farm twelve miles from town and got a job of work at twelve dollars a month. I didn't remain there long though, as I had a chill every other day regular, and therefore couldn't work much.

I made up my mind then to pull for Saint Louis and hunt mother and sister. I had never heard a word from them since they left. After buying a small satchel to put my clothes in and paying for a ticket to the city, I had only twenty-five cents left and part of that I spent for dinner that day.

I arrived in East Saint Louis about midnight with only ten cents left. I wanted to buy a ginger-cake or something as I was very hungry, but hated to as I needed the dime to pay my way across the river next morning. I wasn't very well posted then, in regard to the ways of getting on in the world, or I would have spent the dime for something to eat, and then beat my way across the river.

# 4. MY SECOND EXPERIENCE IN ST. LOUIS

BRIGHT and early next morning I gave my dime to the ferry-man and pulled out for the bustling city, where I was soon lost in the large crowd which thronged the levee.

I left my satchel in a saloon and struck out to find Mr. Socks, hoping he could give me some information as to mother and sister's whereabouts, but I was sadly disappointed, he had left that part of the city in which he lived when I knew him.

I put in the rest of the day gazing through the show windows, especially of the bakeries, at the fat pies, cakes, etc., for I was getting very hungry, my last meal being dinner the day before.

About dark I strolled up to a second-hand book store and asked how much a bible, nearly new, would bring? The man behind the counter told me to bring it around and he would give whatever it was worth. So I struck out after my satchel; I hated the idea of parting with the book for it had been presented to me by my late employer's mother Mrs. Moore, a nice old lady who had taken a liking to me. But you know how it is when a fellow is hungry, or would have known had you been in my shoes.

I got twenty-five cents for the bible and immediately invested fifteen cents of it in a mince pie.

That night I stowed myself away in an empty dry goods box. I did not sleep well, and when I did sleep it was to dream of snakes and other venomous reptiles.

I put in the whole of the next day hunting work, but failed to find it. I had bought a five cent ginger-cake for my dinner and now I got a five cent pie for my supper; this broke me flat and I had nothing else that I could sell; so I put up for the night in a pile of bailed hay, which was stacked up behind a store.

The next morning I struck out again hunting work, but this time on an empty stomach. About two o'clock in the afternoon I found a hack driver who said he wanted to hire a boy to take care of his horses; he said he would not be going home until about one o'clock that night and for me to wait for him in front of the Court house on Fourth street.

Just as soon as dark came, I went to the appointed place and staid there for fear my man would conclude to go home earlier than he expected. I was exceedingly happy when the long-looked for hour drew near, for I thought it wouldn't be long until I would have a good square meal and a warm bed to sleep in.

About two o'clock, while leaning against a lamp-post gazing up and down Fourth street, a policeman punched me in the ribs and told me to "hunt my hole" and that if he caught me out again so late at night he would put me in the cooler.

I pulled out across the street and waited until he got out of sight, then I went back to my same old stand, thinking that my man would certainly be along in a few moments at the outside. Every hack that drove by would cause me to have a spell of the blues, until another hove in sight—soon to disappear again. Finally about three o'clock my courage and what few sparks of hopes that still remained, wilted, for, an empty stomach and sitting up so late had given me a terrible headache, which was almost past endurance. 27

I was sitting on the edge of the sidewalk, with my face buried in both hands, crying, when someone touched me on the shoulder. I was scared at first for I thought it was a "peeler;" but my fears vanished when I looked up into the gleaming countenance of a small, red complexioned man, who said in a pleasant tone:— "Is there anything I can do for you my little man?"

His kindness proved too much for me, I burst out crying and it was quite awhile before I could tell him my trouble. He was terribly mad when I told him how the hack man had served me; he told me to watch for the hard-hearted wretch next day and if I saw him to point him out and he would teach him how to play jokes on innocent children.

He took me to his boarding place, a fancy restaurant, right across the street; he said he was just fixing to go to bed when he spied me across the street, acting as though in trouble.

When he found out that I hadn't had a square meal for three days he remarked that it was a d——d shame and then told the night clerk, who appeared to be half asleep, to have me a good supper fixed up and to give me a good room. He then bid me good night and started to bed, telling me to remain there until I found work, if it was a month, that he would arrange everything with the proprietor in the morning before he went to work. I thanked him with tears in my eyes, for his kindness.

I was so tired and sleepy that I never woke up until nearly noon next day. After eating breakfast, I struck out to hunt a job, but failed as usual.

Three days after, while out hunting work, I stopped an old man and asked him if he knew where I could find a job? He smiled and said: "My boy this is the fourth time you have asked me that same question in the last three days. You must like my looks, for I have noticed you pass scores of men without stopping them."

I told him I never tackled a man unless he had a pleasing

28

countenance, for I had been snapped up short by so many; I also told him that I did not remember asking him before.

He finally, after asking me a few questions, said: "Follow me and I will find you work before I stop."

The first place we went into was the Planters' House, on Fourth street, between Pine and Chestnut, and he asked the clerk if they needed a bell boy. "No," was the short answer he received.

He then asked where he could find the proprietor. "Up in his room, No.—, on first floor," was the answer.

We found the "boss" busily writing. My new friend plead my case like a dutch uncle and told him if I didn't prove to be just what he recommended me to be—a wide-awake, get-up-and-get, honest boy, that he would pay all damages, etc.

That seemed to settle it, for I was told to go down to the office and wait for orders.

I was too happy to live. I thanked the kind old gentleman from the bottom of my heart and offered to pay him for his trouble as soon as I earned some money. He told me I could pay him for his trouble by being a good boy.

After waiting a few minutes in the office, the proprietor came down and made a bargain with me. My wages were to be ten dollars a month. He gave me one month's wages in advance, to buy clean clothes with.

I was put on the forenoon watch which went on duty at eight in the morning and came off at one in the afternoon. There were five of us on at a time.

We would always make from twenty-five cents to five dollars a day while on duty, for we hardly ever went to wait on a person but what they would give us something in the shape of money. Gamblers generally gave us the most; sometimes a lot of them would get together in a room to play cards and send down to the bar after their drinks and may be send a ten or twenty dollar bill and tell the bell boy to keep the change. With this money we used to have some gay old times taking in the city after coming off guard.

The next fall, nearly one year after landing at the "Planters," I had a fight with one of the bell boys, Jimmie Byron. He called me a liar and I jumped aboard of him. When it was over with, the clerk, Mr. Cunningham, called me up to the counter and slapped me without saying a word.

I went right straight to my room, packed up my "gripsack" and went to the proprietor for a settlement.

He was surprised and wanted to know what in the world had gotten into me.

I told him the whole thing, just as it happened. He tried to get me to stay but I was still mad and wouldn't listen to him. I had made up my mind to buy a pistol, come back and get square with Mr. Cunningham for slapping me.

I left the house with eighteen dollars in my pocket; jumped aboard of a street car and rode down to the levee. I left my valise at a saloon and then started back to find a gun store. I finally found one and gave ten dollars for a fancy little ivory handled five-shooter.

I then started for the "Planters" still as mad as an old setting hen. I had not gone far when I came across a large crowd gathered around one of those knife rackets, where you pay a quarter for five rings and try to "ring" a knife.

I watched the thing awhile and finally invested a quarter. I got a little "Jim Crow" barlow the first throw. That made it interesting, so I bought another quarters worth, and another until five dollars was gone. This did not satisfy me, so I kept on until I didn't have a nickel left.

But wasn't I mad when I realized what I had done! I forgot all about my other troubles and felt like breaking my own head instead of Cunningham's.

I went to the levee and found out that the "Bart Able" would start for New Orleans in a few minutes, so I ran to get my satchel, not far off, determined on boarding the steamer and remaining there until kicked off. Anything to get nearer the land of my birth, I thought, even if I had to break the rules of a gentleman in doing so.

When the Purser came around collecting fares, I laid my case before him with tears in my eyes; I told him I was willing to work—and hard, too, to pay my fare. He finally, after studying awhile, said, "Well go ahead, I'll find something for you to do."

Everything went on lovely with me until one evening when we stopped at a landing to take on some freight, mostly grain. We pulled up by the side of an old disabled steamer which was being used for a wharf-boat and went to work loading. The job given to me was sewing sacks when ever one was found out of order.

There were two sets of men loading, one in the stern and the other in the bow, and I was supposed to do the sewing at both ends. When they came across a holey sack, if I happened to be at the other end they would holloa for me and I would go running through the narrow passage way, leading from one end to the other.

I was in the stern when the sound of my name came from the other end; I grabbed my ball of twine and struck out in a dog trot through the passage the sides of which were formed of grain piled to the ceiling. When about half way through I thought I heard my name called from the end I had just left; I stopped to listen and while waiting, being tired, I went to lean over against the wall of sacked grain, but instead of a wall there was an old vacated hatchway and over into that I went. There being no flooring in the boat, there was nothing but the naked timbers for my weary bones to alight upon.

## 5. A NEW EXPERIENCE

THE next day about noon I came to my senses. I found myself all alone in a nice little room on a soft bed. I tried to get up but it was useless; my back felt as if it was broken. I couldn't think what had happened to me. But finally the door opened and in stepped a doctor, who explained the whole matter. He said the captain, just as the boat was fixing to pull out, was walking through the passage way when he heard my groans down in the hold and getting a lantern, ladder and help, fished me out almost lifeless. I was in the captain's private room and having the best of care. The back of my head was swollen out of shape, it having struck on one of the cross timbers, while my back landed across another. The doctor said I owed my life to the captain for finding me, "for," said he, "if you had remained in there twenty minutes longer your case would have been hopeless."

At last we arrived in Memphis, Tenn. We had been traveling very slowly on account of having to stop at all the small landings and unload freight or take on more.

After landing at Memphis I took a notion that a little walk would help my lame back, so I struck out along the river bank, very slowly.

During my walk I came across a drove of small snipe, and having my pistol with me, I shot at them. The pistol report attracted the attention of two boys who were standing not far off. They came over to me, and one of them, the oldest, who was on crutches, having only one leg, asked how much I would take for my "shooter?" I told him I would take ten dollars for it, as I was in need of money. He examined it carefully and then said: "It's a trade buddy, but you will have to go up to that little house yonder, to get the money, as I haven't got that much with me."

The house he pointed out stood off by itself to the right of the town, which was situated about a mile from the river. The house in question being half a mile off, I told him that I was too weak to walk that far, on account of my back being out of whack. "Well," said he, "you go with us as far as that big sand hill yonder," pointing to a large red sand hill a few hundred yards from where we stood, "and my chum here, who has got two good legs, will run on and get the money while we wait."

I agreed, not suspecting anything wrong and when behind the sand hill, out of sight of the steamboat landing, Mr. one-leg threw down on me with my own "shooter" and ordered me to throw up my hands. I obeyed and held mighty still while the other young ruffian went through my pockets. They walked off with everything I had in my pockets, even took my valise key. I felt considerably relieved, I can assure you, when the cocked revolver was taken down from within a few inches of my nose. I was in dread for fear his trembling finger might accidentally touch the trigger.

As soon as I was released I went right back to the landing and notified a policeman who struck out after them. But whether he

33

caught them or not I never knew, as the "Bart Able" steamed down the river shortly afterwards.

The same evening after arriving in New Orleans the "Bart Able" pulled back, for Saint Louis, leaving me there flat broke and among strangers.

I looked terribly blue late that evening as I walked up and down the crowded levee studying what to do. I had already been to the Morgan steamship landing and begged for a chance to work my way to Texas, but met with poor success. I could not hire out even if I had applied and got a job, for my back was still stiff, so much so that I couldn't stoop down without terrible pain.

That night I laid down under an old tarpaulin which was spread over a lot of sugar.

After getting up and shaking the dust off next morning, I went down the river about a mile where scores of small boats were being unloaded.

Among them were several boat loads of oranges, bananas, etc., which were being unloaded. In carrying the bananas on shore the over ripe ones would drop off. On those I made my breakfast, but I wished a thousand times before night that I had not eaten them, for Oh Lord, how my head did ache!

That night I went to sleep on a pile of cotton bales—that is I tried to sleep, but my headache was terrible, I could get but little repose.

The next morning I found there was a Morgan steamship in from Texas, and I struck out to interview the captain in regard to a free ride to Texas. But the old pot-bellied sinner wouldn't talk to me.

In the afternoon I began to grow weak from hunger and my back ached badly. I sat down on an old stove at the foot of Canal street and never moved for three long hours.

Finally a well dressed old man about fifty years of age, with

34

an umbrella over his head, came out of Couens' office, a small building a short distance from where I sat, and walking up to me said, in a gruff voice, "young man what are you sitting out here in the sun for, so upright and stiff, as if nailed to that old stove?"

I told him I was compelled to sit upright on account of a lame back. In fact I laid my case before him in full. He then said in a much more pleasant voice: "My boy I'm going to make you an offer, and you can take it or let it alone—just as you like. I will give you four dollars a month to help my wife around the house and at the end of four months will give you a free pass to Texas. You see I am agent for Couens' Red River line of boats and, therefore, can get a pass cheap."

I accepted his offer at once and thanked him with all my heart for his kindness. Being on his way home, we boarded a Canal street car. It was then almost sundown.

About a half hour's ride brought us within half a block of our destination.

Walking up a pair of nicely finished steps at No. 18 Derbigny street, he rang a bell. A negro servant whom he called "Ann," answered the call. Everything sparkled within, for the house was furnished in grand style. The old gentleman introduced me to his wife as a little Texas hoosier that had strayed off from home and was about to starve.

After supper "Miss Mary," as the servants called Mrs. Myers and as I afterwards called her showed me to the bath house and told me to give myself an extraordinary good scrubbing.

I do not know as this improved my looks any, as I hadn't any clean clothes to put on, my valise having been stolen during my illness coming down the river.

The next day Miss Mary took me to a clothing house and fitted me out in fine style. I admired all but the narrow brimmed hat and peaked toed gaiters. I wanted a broad brimmed hat and star top boots, but she said I would look too much like a hoosier with them on.

That evening I got a black eye. After Mr. Myers came home from his work about four o'clock, we all went out on the front steps to breathe the fresh air. There being a crowd of boys playing at the corner I asked Mr. and Mrs. Myers if I could go over and watch them awhile. Both consented, but told me not to stay long as they didn't want me to get into the habit of mixing with the street loafers.

On arriving there all eyes were turned towards me. One fellow yelled out, "Hello dandy, when did you arrive!" and another one remarked, "He is a stiff cuss—ain't he?"

I concluded there was nothing to be seen and turned back; just as I turned around a yellow negro boy slipped up behind me and pulled my hair. The white boys had put him up to it, no doubt.

I jumped aboard of him quicker than a flash and forgot all about my sore back. It was nip and tuck for awhile—we both being about the same size, but I finally got him down and blooded his nose in good shape. As I went to get up he kicked me over one eye with his heavy boot. Hence the black eye, which was swollen up in a few minutes to an enormous size.

I expected to get a scolding from Mr. and Mrs. Myers, but they both gloried in my spunk for taking my own part. They had witnessed the whole thing.

Somehow or another that fight took the kink out of my back for from that time on it began to get well. I am bothered with it though, to this day, when I take cold or do a hard day's work.

# 6. ADOPTED AND SENT TO SCHOOL

MR. AND MRS. MYERS had no children and after I had been with them about a month, they proposed to adopt me, or at least they made me promise to stay with them until I was twenty-one years of age.

They were to send me to school until I was seventeen and then start me in business. They also promised to give me everything they had at their death.

So they prepared me for school right away. As I was not very far advanced in book learning, having forgotten nearly all that Mr. Hale taught me, they thought I had better go to Fisk's public school until I got a start.

I had not been going to this school long when I had trouble with the lady teacher, Miss Finnely. It happened thus: A boy sitting behind me, struck me on the neck with a slate pencil, and when I turned around and accused him of it he whispered, "you lie." I gave him a lick on the nose that made him bawl like a calf.

Of course the teacher heard it and called us up to take our medicine.

She made the other boy hold out his hand first and after giving him five raps told him to take his seat.

It was then my time, and I stuck out my hand like a little man. She gave me five licks and was raising the rule to strike again when I jerked my hand away, at the same time telling her that it wasn't fair to punish me the most when the other boy caused the fuss. She insisted on giving me a little more so finally I held out my hand and received five more licks and still she was not satisfied; but I was and went to my seat. She told me two or three times to come back but I would not do it, so she sent a boy upstairs after Mr. Dyer, the gentleman who taught the large boys.

I had seen Mr. Dyer try his hand on boys, at several different times, therefore didn't intend to let him get hold of me if I could help it. She saw me looking towards the door, so she came over and stood between me and it.

I heard Mr. Dyer coming down the stairs; that was enough; I flew for the door. I remember running against something soft and knocking it over and suppose it must have been Miss Finnely. When I got to the street I pulled straight for home.

About a week afterwards Mr. Myers sent me to pay school, where I was taught German, French and English. My teacher was an old gentleman who only took a few select scholars.

Everything went on fine until the following spring, in May or June, when I got into a fuss with one of the scholars and skipped the country.

The way it happened: One day when school let out for dinner we all, after emptying our dinner baskets, struck out for the "green" to play "foot and a half."

There was one boy in the crowd by the name of Stemcamp who was always trying to pick a fuss with me. He was twice as large as I was, therefore I tried to avoid him, but this time he called me a liar and I made for him.

During the scuffle which followed, I got out my little pearl handled knife, one "Miss Mary" had given me just a few days before and was determined to use it the first opportunity.

I was down on all fours and he astride of my back putting it to me in the face, underhanded. The only place I could get at with the knife was his legs, so I stuck it in up to the handle, on the inside of one leg, just below the groin and ripped down.

He jumped ten feet in the air and roared out "Holy Moses!"

As soon as I regained my feet he took to his heels, but I soon overtook him and got another dig at his back. I thought sure I had done him up for good this time but found out afterwards that I had done no harm, with the exception of ripping his clothes down the back.

The next day at that time I was on my way to Saint Louis. I had stowed myself away on board of the "Mollie Able" among the cotton bales.

The second night out we had a blow up. One of the cylinder-heads blew out of the engine. It nearly killed the engineer and fireman, also several other persons.

A little negro boy—who was stealing his passage—and I were sleeping on a pile of lumber close to the engine when she went off. We both got pretty badly scalded.

The steamer ran ashore and laid there until morning and then went the balance of the way on one wheel. It took us just eight days from that time to get to Saint Louis.

I remained in Saint Louis one day without food—not caring to visit the "Planters" or any of my acquaintances—and then walked to Lebanon, Ill., twenty-five miles. I thought may be I might find out through some of my Lebanon friends where mother and sister were.

It was nearly noon when I struck out on my journey and nine o'clock at night when I arrived at my destination. I went straight to Mrs. Bell's, where sister had worked, but failed to hear a word of mother and sister's whereabouts.

Mrs. Bell gave me a good bed that night and next morning I struck out to hunt a job.

After considerable tramping around I found work with one

39

of my old employers, a Mr. Jacobs, who lived twelve miles from town.

I only worked a short while when I began to wish I was back under "Miss Mary's" wing. So one morning I quit and pulled for Saint Louis.

I had money enough to pay my fare to Saint Louis and I arrived there just as the "Robert E. Lee" and "Natchez" were fixing to pull out on their big race for New Orleans.

The "Robert E. Lee" being my favorite boat, I jumped aboard just as she was shoving off. Of course I had to keep hidden most of the time, especially when the captain or purser were around. I used to get my chuck from the cook who thought I was a bully boy.

The "Natchez" would have beaten, no doubt, but she got too smart by trying to make a cut-off through an old canal opposite Memphis and got stuck in the mud.

The first thing after landing in New Orleans, I hunted up one of my boy friends and found out by him how my victim was getting on. He informed me that he was up and hobbling about on crutches. He also stated that the poor fellow came very near losing his leg. I concluded if they did have me arrested that Mr. Myers was able to help me out, so I braced up and struck out for home.

Mr. and Mrs. Myers were terribly tickled over my return. They had an awful time though getting me scrubbed up again, as I was very black and dirty.

A few days after my return Mr. Myers went to see my same old teacher to find out whether he would take me back or not. At first he said that no money could induce him to be bothered with me again, but finally Mr. Myers talked him into the notion of trying me once more.

So the next morning I shouldered my books and struck out for school to take up my same old studies, German, French and English.

# 7. BACK AT LAST TO THE LONE STAR STATE

E VERYTHING went on lovely until the coming fall, about the latter part of November when I skipped the country for good. I will tell you how it happened.

One afternoon a fire broke out close to the school house and as everybody was rushing by, I became excited and wanted to go too, to see the fun. I asked the teacher if I could go, but he refused in a gruff voice. This did not keep me, I made a break for the door and was soon lost among the surging mass of people.

The next heard of me was on the "rolling deep." I had boarded a Morgan steamship and stowed myself away until the vessel was at sea, where I knew they wouldn't land to put me ashore.

"St. Mary" was the name of the ship. She lost one of her wheel houses and was considerably out of shape when we landed in Galveston, Texas. It had stormed terribly during the whole trip.

During the few hours that the ship remained in Galveston, I put in my time hunting an old uncle of mine by the name of "Nick" White, whom I had never seen. He had been living there seventeen years, therefore I experienced but little difficulty in finding his place; but after finding it I didn't have courage enough to go in and make myself known. One reason was, I thought he

41

might think I was beholden to him, or in other words, trying to get his sympathy. I just stood at the gate a few minutes viewing the beautiful shrubbery, which filled the spacious yard and went back to the boat which by that time, was just fixing to pull out.

We arrived in Indianola one morning about sun-up. I recognized several of my old acquaintances standing on the wharf before the ship landed; among them was my old God-father Mr. Hagerty, who stood for me when I was being christened by the Catholic priest.

They were all surprised to see me back. Mr. Hagerty took me home with him and told me to content myself until I could find work.

In about a week I went to work for Mr. H. Selickson, who ran a packing house five miles below town. He gave me fifteen dollars a month all winter.

The first month's wages went for a fancy pistol, the next, or at least part of it, for a pair of star topped boots and all the balance on "monte," a mexican game. There were lots of mexicans working there and after working hours some of them would "deal" monte while the rest of us "bucked."

About the first of February I quit the packing house and went to Matagorda where I was welcomed by all my old acquaintances. From there I took a trip over to the "Settlement," on the Peninsula, to see the old homestead. Everything looked natural; the cedar and fig trees were covered with little red winged black birds, seemingly the same ones that were there when I left, nearly three years before.

After a week's stay in the Settlement, I went back to Matagorda and went to work for Mr. Joseph Yeamans, a Baptist preacher. My work was farming and my wages part of the crop.

Mr. Yeamans' farm was a thirty acre sand patch on the Peninsula, about forty miles above the Settlement. Our aim was to raise a big crop of water melons and sweet potatoes, but when I

42

left everything pointed to a big crop of grass burrs and a very slim lay out of sweet potatoes and water melons.

The old gentleman and I lived all alone in a little delapidated shanty with a dirt floor. Our chuck consisted of black coffee, hard-tack and coon or 'possum meat. We had three good coon dogs, therefore had plenty of fresh meat such as it was.

There being plenty "Mavricks" close at hand, and being tired of coon meat, I used to try and get the old man to let me butcher one now and then for a change, but he thought it wicked to kill cattle not our own.

As some of you may not know what a "Mavrick" is, I will try and explain.

In early days, a man by the name of Mavrick settled on the Lavaca river and started a cow ranch. He being a chicken-hearted old rooster, wouldn't brand nor ear-mark any of his cattle. All his neighbors branded theirs, therefore Mr. Mavrick claimed everything that wore long ears.

When the war broke out Mr. Mavrick had to bid adieu to wife and babies and go far away to fight for his country's good.

When the cruel war was ended, he went home and found his cattle roaming over a thousand hills. Everywhere he went he could see thousands upon thousands of his long-eared cattle.

But when his neighbors and all the men in the surrounding country came home and went to branding their five years increase, Mr. Mavrick did not feel so rich. He made a terrible fuss about it, but it did no good, as in a very few years his cattle wore some enterprising man's brand and he was left out in the cold.

Hence the term "Mavrick." At first people used to say: "Yonder goes one of Mr. Mavrick's animals!" Now they say: "Yonder goes a Mavrick!"

About the time we got our crops, sweet potatoes, melons, etc., in the ground, I swore off farming and skipped out for town, leaving Mr. Yeamans my share of the "crop" free *gratis*.

After arriving in Matagorda I hired out to a Mr. Tom Nie, who was over there, from Rancho Grande, hiring some Cow Boys.

"Rancho Grande" was owned by "Shanghai" Pierce and Allen and at that time was considered one of the largest ranches in the whole state of Texas. To give you an idea of its size, will state, that the next year after I went to work we branded twenty-five thousand calves—that is, just in one season.

Altogether there were five of us started to Rancho Grande to work—all boys about my own age; we went in a sail boat to Palacious Point, where the firm had an outside ranch and where they were feeding a large lot of cow ponies for spring work.

It was about the middle of April, 1871, that we all, about twenty of us, pulled out for the headquarter ranch at the head of Tresspalacious creek. It took us several days to make the trip as we had to brand calves and Mavricks on the way up.

A few days after arriving at the ranch Mr. or "Old Shang" Pierce as he was commonly called, arrived from Old Mexico with about three hundred head of wild spanish ponies, therefore we kids had a high old time learning the art of riding a "pitching" horse.

We put in several days at the ranch making preparations to start out on a two months trip. Being a store there we rigged up in good shape; I spent two or three months' wages for an outfit, spurs, etc., trying to make myself look like a thoroughbred Cow Boy from Bitter Creek.

There were three crowds of us started at the same time; one to work up the Colorado river, the other around home and the third which was ours, to work west in Jackson and Lavaca counties.

Our crowd consisted of fifteen men, one hundred head of ponies—mostly wild ones—and a chuck wagon loaded down with coffee, flour, molasses and salt. Tom Nie was our boss.

## 8. LEARNING TO ROPE WILD STEERS

Arriving on the Navadad river, we went to work gathering a herd of "trail" beeves and also branding Mavricks at the same time. Some days we would brand as high as three or four hundred Mavricks—none under two years old.

After about a month's hard work we had the herd of eleven hundred ready to turn over to Mr. Black who had bought them, delivered to him at the Snodgrass ranch. They were all old mossy horn fellows, from seven to twenty-seven years old.

Mr. Black was a Kansas "short horn" and he had brought his outfit of "short horn" men and horses, to drive the herd "up the trail."

Some of the men had never seen a Texas steer, consequently they crossed Red river into the Indian territory with nothing left but the "grub" wagon and horses. They had lost every steer and Mr. Black landed in Kansas flat broke.

Lots of the steers came back to their old ranges and Mr. "Shanghai" had the fun of selling them over again, to some other greeny, may be.

"Shanghai" Pierce went to Kansas the next year and when he returned he told of having met Mr. Black up there, working at his old trade—blacksmithing. He said Mr. Black cursed Texas shamefully and swore that he never would, even if he should live to be as old as Isaac, son of Jacob, dabble in long horns again.

After getting rid of Mr. Black's herd we turned our whole attention to branding Mavricks.

About the first of August we went back to the ranch and found that it had changed hands in our absence. "Shanghai" Pierce and his brother Jonathan had sold out their interests to Allen, Pool & Co. for the snug little sum of one hundred and ten thousand dollars.

That shows what could be done in those days, with no capital, but lots of cheek and a branding iron. The two Pierce's had come out there from Yankeedom a few years before poorer than skimmed milk.

Everything had taken a change—even to the ranch. It had been moved down the river four miles to Mr. John Moore's place. Mr. Moore had been appointed "big chief," hence the ranch being moved to his place.

About the middle of August we pulled out again with a fresh supply of horses, six to the man and a bran new boss, Mr. Wiley Kuykendall.

Some of the boys hated to part with Mr. Nie, but I was glad of the change, for he wouldn't allow me to rope large steers nor fight when I got on the war-path. I remember one time he gave me fits for laying a negro out with a four-year old club; and another time he laid me out with his open hand for trying to carve one of the boys up with a butcher knife.

We commenced work about the first of September on "Big Sandy" in Lavaca county, a place noted for wild "brush" cattle. Very few people lived in that section, hence so many wild unbranded cattle.

To illustrate the class of people who lived on Big Sandy, will relate a little picnic a negro and I had a few days after our arrival there.

46

While herding a bunch of cattle, gathered the day before, on a small prairie, we noticed a footman emerge from the thick timber on the opposite side from where we were and make straight for a spotted pony that was "hobbled" and grazing out in the open space.

He was indeed a rough looking customer, being half naked. He had nothing on his head but a thick mat of almost gray hair; and his feet and legs were bare.

We concluded to "rope" him and take him to camp, so taking down our ropes and putting spurs to our tired horses we struck out.

He saw us coming and only being about a hundred yards from the spotted pony, he ran to him and cutting the "hobbles," which held his two front legs together, jumped aboard of him and was off in the direction he had just come, like a flash. The pony must have been well trained for he had nothing to guide him with.

A four hundred yard race for dear life brought him to the "brush"—that is timber, thickly covered with an underbrush of live-oak "runners." He shot out of sight like an arrow. He was not a minute too soon, for we were right at his heels.

We gave up the chase after losing sight of him, for we couldn't handle our ropes in the "brush."

The next day the camp was located close to the spot where he disappeared at, and several of us followed up his trail. We found him and his three grown daughters, his wife having died a short while before, occupying a little one room log shanty in a lonely spot about two miles from the little prairie in which we first saw him. The whole outfit were tough looking citizens. The girls had never seen a town, so they said. They had about two acres in cultivation and from that they made their living. Their nearest neighbor was a Mr. Penny, who lived ten miles west and the nearest town was Columbus, on the Colorado river, fifty miles east.

As the cattle remained hidden out in the "brush" during the day-time, only venturing out on the small prairies at night, we had to do most of our work early in the morning, commencing an hour or two before daylight. As you might wish to know exactly how we did, will try and explain:—About two hours before daylight the cook would holloa "chuck," and then Mr. Wiley would go around and yell "breakfast, boys; d——n you get up!" two or three times in our ears.

Breakfast being over we would saddle up our ponies, which had been staked out the night before, and strike out for a certain prairie may be three or four miles off—that is all but two or three men, just enough to bring the herd, previously gathered, on as soon as it became light enough to see.

Arriving at the edge of the prairie we would dismount and wait for daylight.

At the first peep of day the cattle, which would be out in the prairie, quite a distance from the timber, would all turn their heads and commence grazing at a lively rate towards the nearest point of timber. Then we would ride around through the brush, so as not to be seen, until we got to the point of timber that they were steering for.

When it became light enough to see good, we would ride out, rope in hand, to meet them and apt as not one of the old-timers, may be a fifteen or twenty-year old steer, which were continuously on the lookout, would spy us before we got twenty yards from the timber. Then the fun would begin—the whole bunch, may be a thousand head, would stampede and come right towards us. They never were known to run in the opposite direction from the nearest point of timber. But with cattle raised on the prairies, it's the reverse, they will always leave the timber.

After coming in contact, every man would rope and tie down one of the finest animals in the bunch. Once in awhile some fellow would get more beef than he could manage; under those

48

circumstances he would have to worry along until some other fellow got through with his job and came to his rescue.

If there was another prairie close by we would go to it and tie down a few more, but we would have to get there before sunup or they would all be in the brush. It was their habit to graze out into the little prairies at night-fall and go back to the brush by sunrise next morning.

Finally the herd which we had gathered before and which was already "broke in," would arrive from camp, where we had been night-herding them and then we would drive it around to each one of the tied-down animals, letting him up so he couldn't help from running right into the herd, where he would generally stay contented. Once in awhile though, we would strike an old steer that couldn't be made to stay in the herd. Just as soon as he was untied and let up he would go right through the herd and strike for the brush, fighting his way. Under those circumstances we would have to sew up their eyes with a needle and thread. That would bring them to their milk, as they couldn't see the timber.

I got into several scrapes on this trip, by being a new hand at the business. One time I was going at full speed and threw my rope onto a steer just as he got to the edge of the timber; I couldn't stop my horse in time, therefore the steer went on one side of a tree and my horse on the other and the consequence was, my rope being tied hard and fast to the saddle-horn, we all landed up against the tree in a heap.

At another time, on the same day, I roped a large animal and got my horse jerked over backwards on top of me and in the horse getting up he got me all wound up in the rope, so that I couldn't free myself until relieved by "Jack" a negro man who was near at hand. I was certainly in a ticklish predicament that time; the pony was wild and there I hung fast to his side with my head down while the steer, which was still fastened to the rope, was making every effort to gore us.      49

Just before Christmas Moore selected our outfit to do the shipping at Palacious Point, where a Morgan steamship landed twice a week to take on cattle for the New Orleans market.

We used to ship about five hundred head at each shipping. After getting rid of one bunch we would strike right back, to meet one of the gathering outfits, after another herd. There were three different outfits to do the gathering for us.

We kept that up all winter and had a tough time of it, too, as it happened to be an unusually cold and wet winter.

Towards spring the cattle began to get terribly poor, so that during the cold nights while night-herding them a great many would get down in the mud and freeze to death. Have seen as high as fifty head of dead ones scattered over the ground where the herd had drifted during the night. It's a pity if such nights as those didn't try our nerves.

Sometimes it would be twelve o'clock at night before we would get the cattle loaded aboard of the ship. But when we did get through we would surely have a picnic—filling up on Mr. Geo. Burkheart's red eye. Mr. Burkheart kept a store at the "Point" well filled with Cow Boys delight—in fact he made a specialty of the stuff.

Our camping ground was three miles from the Point, and some mornings the cook would get up and find several saddled horses standing around camp waiting for their corn—their riders having fallen by the wayside.

# 9. OWNING MY FIRST CATTLE

WHEN spring opened, our outfit, under the leadership of Mr. Robert Partin, Mr. Wiley having quit, struck out up the Colorado river in Whorton and Colorado counties to brand Mavricks.

About the last of July we went to the "home" ranch, where Mr. Wiley was put in charge of us again. We were sent right out on another trip, west, to Jackson county.

It was on this trip that I owned my first cattle. Mr. Wiley concluded it would look more business like if he would brand a few Mavricks for himself instead of branding them all for Allen, Pool & Co., so he began putting his own brand on all the finest looking ones. To keep us boys from giving him away, he gave us a nest egg apiece—that is a few head to draw to. My nest eggs were a couple of two-year olds, and my brand was A. T. connected—the T. on top of the A. Of course after that I always carried a piece of iron tied to my saddle so in case I got off on the prairie by myself I could brand a few Mavricks for myself, without Mr. Wiley being any the wiser of it. The way I would go about it would be to rope and tie down one of the long-eared fellows and after heating the straight piece of round, iron bolt, in the brush or "cow-chip" fire, "run" my brand on his hip or ribs. He was then my property.

Everything ran along as smooth as if on greased wheels for about two months, when somehow or another, Mr. Moore, our big chief, heard of our little private racket and sent for us to come home.

Mr. Wiley got the "G. B." at once and a Mr. Logan was put in his place. Now this man Logan was a very good man but he was out of his latitude, he should have been a second mate on a Mississippi steamboat.

I worked with Logan one trip, until we got back to the ranch and then I settled up for the first time since going to work, nearly two years before.

An old irishman by the name of "Hunky-dorey" Brown kept the store and did the settling up with the men. When he settled with me he laid all the money, in silver dollars, that I had earned since commencing work, which amounted to a few hundred dollars, out on the counter and then after eyeing me awhile, said: "Allen, Pool & Co. owe you three hundred dollars," or whatever the amount was, "and you owe Allen, Pool & Co. two hundred ninety-nine dollars and a quarter, which leaves you seventy-five cents." He then raked all but six bits into the money drawer.

To say that I felt mortified wouldn't near express my feelings. I thought the whole pile was mine and therefore had been figuring on the many purchases that I intended making. My intentions were to buy a herd of ponies and go to speculating. I had a dozen or two ponies, that I knew were for sale, already picked out in my mind. But my fond expectations were soon trampled under foot. You see I had never kept an account, consequently never knew how I stood with the company.

After pocketing my six bits, I mounted "Fannie" a little mare that I had bought not long before and struck out for W. B.

Grimes' ranch, a few miles up the river. I succeeded in getting a job from the old gentleman at fifteen dollars per month.

Mr. Grimes had a slaughter house on his ranch where he killed cattle for their hides and tallow—the meat he threw to the hogs. About two hundred head per day was an average killing. Did you ask kind reader, if those were all his own cattle that he butchered? If so, will have to say that I never tell tales out of school.

After working around the ranch a short while Mr. Grimes gave me the job of taking care of his "stock horses," that is mares, colts and horses that wern't in use. There were about two hundred head of those and they were scattered in two hundred and fifty different places—over fifty square miles of territory and of course before I could take care of them I had to go to work and gather them up into one bunch.

A little circumstance happened shortly after going to work at the "W. B. G." ranch which I am going to relate.

An old gentleman by the name of Kinchlow, who owned a large horse ranch up on the Colorado river in Whorton county, came down and told Mr. Grimes that his outfit was fixing to start on a horse "hunt" and for him to send a man along, as there were quite a number of "W. B. G." horses in that country.

As I had the job taking care of the horses, it fell to my lot to accompany the old gentleman, Mr. Kinchlow, to his ranch fifty miles distant.

It was bright and early one morning when we pulled out, aiming to ride the fifty miles by ten o'clock that night. Mr. Kinchlow was mounted on "old Beauregard," a large chestnut sorrel, while I rode a fiery little bay.

Our journey was over a bald, wet prairie; night overtook us at the head of Blue creek, still twenty miles from our destination.

A few minutes after crossing Blue creek, just about dusk, we ran across a large panther, which jumped up out of the tall grass in front of us. It was a savage looking beast and appeared to be on the war-path. After jumping to one side it just sat still, growling and showing its ugly teeth. I started to shoot it but Mr. Kinchlow begged me not to as it would frighten his horse, who was then almost beyond control, from seeing the panther.

We rode on and a few minutes afterwards discovered the panther sneaking along after us through the tall grass. I begged Mr. Kinchlow to let me kill it, but he wouldn't agree, as, he said, a pistol shot would cause old Beauregard to jump out of his hide.

It finally became very dark; our guide was a certain bright little star. We had forgotten all about the panther as it had been over half an hour since we had seen it. The old man was relating an indian tale, which made my hair almost stand on end, as I imagined that I was right in the midst of a wild band of reds, when all at once old Beauregard gave a tremendous loud snort and dashed straight ahead at a break-neck speed. Mr. Kinchlow yelled "whoa," every jump; finally his voice died out and I could hear nothing but the sound of his horse's hoofs, and finally the sound of them too, died out.

Of course I socked spurs to my pony and tried to keep up, for I imagined there were a thousand and one indians and panthers right at my heels.

After running about a quarter of a mile I heard something like a faint, human groan, off to my right about fifty yards. I stopped and listened, but could not hear anything more, except now and then the lonely howl of a coyote off in the distance. I finally began to feel lonesome, so I put spurs to my pony again. But I hadn't gone only a few jumps when I checked up and argued with myself thusly:—Now suppose that groan came from the lips of Mr. Kinchlow, who may-be fell from his horse and is badly hurt; then wouldn't it be a shame to run off and leave him there to die when may be a little aid from me would save him?

I finally spunked up and drawing my pistol started in the direction from whence came the groan. My idea in drawing the pistol was, for fear the panther, who I felt satisfied had been the cause of the whole trouble, might tackle me. Suffice it to say that I found the old gentleman stretched out on the ground apparently lifeless and that a half hour's nursing brought him to. He finally after several trials, got so he could stand up, with my aid. I then helped him into my saddle, while I rode behind and held him on and we continued our journey both on one horse. He informed me after he came to his right senses, that old Beauregard had fallen and rolled over him.

We landed at our destination about ten o'clock next morning; but the good old man only lived about two weeks afterwards. He died from the effects of the fall, so I heard.

About Christmas I quit Mr. Grimes and went to work on my own hook, skinning "dead" cattle and adding to the nest egg Mr. Wiley gave me. I put my own brand on quite a number of Mavricks while taking care of Mr. Grimes' horses, which began to make me feel like a young cattle king. The only trouble was they were scattered over too much wild territory and mixed up with so many other cattle. When a fellow branded a Mavrick in those days it was a question whether he would ever see or realize a nickel for it. For just think, one, or even a hundred head mixed up with over a million of cattle, and those million head scattered over a territory one hundred miles square and continually drifting around from one place to another.

After leaving Daddy Grimes I made my home at Mr. Horace Yeamans', an old mexican war veteran, who lived five miles from Grimes'. His family consisted of two daughters and two sons, all grown but the youngest daughter, Sally, who was only fourteen, and who I was casting sheeps eyes at. The old gentleman had brought his children up very pious, which was a glorious thing for me as, during the two years that I made my home there, I got broke of swearing—a dirty, mean habit which had fastened itself upon me, and which I thought was impossible to get rid of. I had become so that it was almost an impossibility for me to utter a sentence without using an oath to introduce it and another to end it. To show how the habit was fastened upon me: Mr. Parten, one of my former bosses, made me an offer of three dollars more wages, on the month, if I would quit cursing but I wouldn't do it.

Horace Yeamans, who was about my own age and I went into partnership in the skinning business. Cattle died by the thousands that winter, on account of the country being overstocked, therefore Horace and I had a regular picnic skinning, and branding Mavricks—only those that looked as if they might pull through the winter.

To give you an idea how badly cattle died that winter will state that, at times, right after a sleet, a man could walk on dead animals for miles without stepping on the ground. This, of course, would be along the Bay shore, where they would pile up on top of one another, not being able to go further, on account of the water.

About five miles east of Mr. Yeamans' was a slough or creek called "Turtle bayou" which lay east and west a distance of several miles, and which I have seen bridged over with dead cattle, from one end to the other. You see the solid mass of half starved animals, in drifting ahead of a severe "Norther," would undertake to cross the bayou, which was very boggy and consequently the weakest ones would form a bridge for the others to cross on.

My share of the first hides we shipped to Indianola amounted to one hundred and fourteen dollars. You bet I felt rich. I never had so much money in all my life. I went at once and bought me a twenty-seven dollar saddle and sent mother twenty-five dollars. I had found out mother's address, in Saint Louis, by one of my old Peninsula friends getting a letter from sister.

Our next sale amounted to more than the first. That time Horace and I went to Indianola with the hides for we wanted to blow in some of our surplus wealth; we were getting too rich.

When spring opened I bought five head of horses and thought I would try my hand at trading horses. The first trade I made, I cleared twenty-five dollars. I gave an old mare which cost me twenty dollars, for a pony which I sold a few days afterwards for forty-five.

Along in May I fell head over heels in love, for the first time in my life. A pretty little fourteen year old Miss, cousin to Horace and the girls, came over on a month's visit and when she left I was completely rattled—couldn't think of anything but her; her beautiful image was continually before my eyes.

Her father, who was Sheriff of Matagorda county lived on the road to Matagorda, fifteen miles from Mr. Yeamans', therefore, during the coming summer I went to town pretty often; to get a new brand recorded was generally my excuse. You see, as she lived about half way between the Yeamans' ranch and town, I could be near her two nights each trip, one going and one returning.

I had very poor success that summer in my new enterprise, horse trading. I was too badly "locoed" to tell a good horse from a bad one; in fact I wasn't fit for anything, unless it would have been a Mail carrier between "Denning's Bridge" and Matagorda.

# 10. A START UP THE CHISHOLM TRAIL

I PUT in the following winter branding Mavricks, skinning cattle and making regular trips to Matagorda; I still remained in partnership with Horace Yeamans in the skinning business. I made considerable money that winter as I sold a greater number of Mavricks than ever before. But the money did me no good as I spent it freely.

That coming spring, it being 1874, I hired to Leander Ward of Jackson county to help gather a herd of steers for the Muckleroy Bros., who were going to drive them to Kansas. I had also made a contract with Muckleroy's boss, Tom Merril, to go up the trail with him, therefore I bid my friends good-bye, not expecting to see them again until the coming fall. My wages were thirty-five dollars per month and all expenses, including railroad fare back home.

After a month's hard work we had the eleven hundred head of wild and woolly steers ready to turn over to the Muckleroy outfit at Thirteen mile point on the Mustang, where they were camped, ready to receive them. Their outfit consisted mostly of Kansas "short horns" which they had brought back with them the year before.

It was a cold, rainy evening when the cattle were counted and turned over to Tom Merril. Henry Coats, Geo. Gifford and myself were the only boys who were turned over with the herd—that is kept right on. We were almost worn out standing night guard half of every night for the past month and then starting in with a fresh outfit made it appear tough to us.

That night it began to storm terribly. The herd began to drift early and by midnight we were five or six miles from camp. The steers showed a disposition to stampede but we handled them easy and sang melodious songs which kept them quieted. But about one o'clock they stampeded in grand shape. One of the "short horns," a long legged fellow by the name of Saint Clair got lost from the herd and finally when he heard the singing came dashing through the herd at full speed yelling "let 'em slide, we'll stay with 'em!" at every jump.

They did slide sure enough, but he failed to "stay with 'em." For towards morning one of the boys came across him lying in the grass sound asleep. When he came dashing through the herd a stampede followed; the herd split up into a dozen different bunches—each bunch going in a different direction. I found myself all alone with about three hundred of the frightened steers. Of course all I could do was to keep in front or in the lead and try to check them up. I finally about three o'clock got them stopped and after singing a few "lullaby" songs they all lay down and went to snoring.

After the last steer dropped down I concluded I would take a little nap too, so locking both legs around the saddle-horn and lying over on the tired pony's rump, with my left arm for a pillow, while the other still held the bridle-reins, I fell asleep. I hadn't slept long though when, from some unaccountable reason, every steer jumped to his feet at the same instant and was off like a flash. My pony which was sound asleep too, I suppose, became frightened and dashed off at full speed in the opposite direction. Of course I was also frightened and hung to the saddle with a death grip. I was unable to raise myself up as the pony was going so fast, therefore had to remain as I was, until after about a mile's run I got him checked up.

Just as soon as I got over my scare I struck out in a gallop in the direction I thought the cattle had gone, but failed to overtake them. I landed in camp almost peetered out about nine o'clock next morning. The rest of the boys were all there, just eating their breakfast. Tom Merril and Henry Coats had managed to hold about half of the herd, while the balance were scattered and mixed up with "range" cattle for twenty miles around.

After eating our breakfast and mounting fresh horses we struck out to gather up the lost steers. We could tell them from the range cattle by the fresh "road" brand—a brand that had been put on a few days before—therefore, by four o'clock that evening we had all but about one hundred head back to camp and those Leander Ward bought back at half price—that is he just bought the road brand or all cattle that happened to be left behind.

On arriving at camp, we all caught fresh horses before stopping to eat dinner or supper, whichever you like to call it, it being then nearly night. The pony I caught was a wild one and after riding up to camp and dismounting to eat dinner, he jerked loose from me and went a flying with my star-spangled saddle.

I mounted a pony belonging to one of the other boys and went in hot pursuit. I got near enough once to throw my rope over his rump and that was all. After a run of fifteen miles I gave it up as a bad job and left him still headed for the Rio Grande.

I got back to camp just at dark and caught a fresh horse before stopping to eat my supper. It was still raining and had kept it up all day long. Mr. "Jim" Muckleroy had an extra saddle along therefore I borrowed it until I could get a chance to buy me another one.

After eating a cold supper, the rain having put the fire out, I mounted and went on "guard," the first part of the night, until one o'clock, being my regular time to stay with the herd, while the last "guard" remained in camp and slept.

About ten o'clock it began to thunder and lightning, which caused the herd to become unruly. Every time a keen clash of thunder would come the herd would stampede and run for a mile or two before we could get them to stop. It continued in that way all night so that we lost another night's rest; but we managed to "stay with 'em" this time; didn't even lose a steer.

That morning we struck out on the trail for Kansas. Everything went on smoothly with the exception of a stampede now and then and a fuss with Jim Muckleroy, who was a regular old sore-head. Charlie, his brother was a white man. Where the trouble began, he wanted Coats and I, we being the only ones in the crowd who could ride wild horses—or at least who were willing to do so, to do the wild horse riding for nothing. We finally bolted and told him that we wouldn't ride another wild horse except our regular "mount," unless he gave us extra pay. You see he expected us to ride a horse a few times until he began to get docile and then turn him over to one of his muley pets while we caught up a fresh one.

At High Hill in Fayette county I got the bounce from old Jim and a little further on Coats got the same kind of a dose; while nearing the northern state-line Geo. Gifford and Tom Merril, the boss, were fired; so that left old Jim in full charge. He hired other men in our places. He arrived in Wichita, Kansas with eight hundred steers, out of the eleven hundred we started with.

After leaving the outfit I rode to the Sunset railroad at Shusenburg and boarded a train for Columbus on the Colorado river. "Pat" Muckleroy, Charlie's son, who was about eighteen years old, quit and went with me. His home was in Columbus and he persuaded me to accompany him and have a good time.

On arriving in Columbus I went with Pat to his home where I remained during my stay in that place. I found Mrs. M., Pat's mother, to be a kind-hearted old lady, and I never shall forget the big, fat apple cobblers she used to make; she could beat the world making them. There were also two young Misses in the family, Nannie and Mary, who made time pass off pleasantly with me.

It being seventy-five miles to Tresspalacious and there being no railroad nearer than that, I had to wait for a chance to get home. I could have bought a horse and saddle when I first struck town but after remaining there a week I began to get light in the pocket, for it required quite a lot of money to keep up my end with the crowd that Pat associated with.

At last after about a three weeks stay, I struck Asa Dawdy, an old friend from Tresspalacious. He was there with a load of stock and was just fixing to load them on the cars to ship them to Galveston when I ran afoul of him. He had sold his saddle and was going to put his pet pony, one that he wouldn't sell, into a pasture until some other time when he happend up there. So you see I was in luck, he turned the pony over to me to ride home on.

After buying and rigging up a saddle I left town flat broke. I spent my last dime for a glass of lemonade just before leaving. Thus ended my first experience on the "trail."

## 11. BUYS A BOAT AND BECOMES A SAILOR

A THREE days' ride brought me to Grimes' ranch where I hoped to strike a job, but the old gent' informed me that he was full handed—had more men than he really needed. But he offered me a job cutting cord wood at a dollar a cord until there should be an opening for me, which he thought would be when the branding outfit arrived from Jackson county where it had gone quite a while before.

"Cutting cord wood" sounded tough to me, but I finally agreed to try it a round or two, for I hated the idea of being "busted." Mr. Grimes was to advance me about two weeks provisions on "tick," so I concluded I couldn't lose anything—unless it was a few pounds of muscle and I had grave doubts about that, for I knew my failing when it came to dabbling in wood.

Before launching out into the wood business I borrowed a horse and struck out to hunt up old Satan so that I could ride around and find easy trees to cut down; I found him about thirty miles from Grimes' ranch; he was fat and wild; I had to get help to put him in a corral and when I mounted him he pitched like a wolf. He had forgotten that he had ever been ridden.

The "wood camp" was three miles from the ranch in a thinly timbered bottom. I had to camp all by myself, which made it a disagreeable job.

The first day, after locating camp, was spent in building a kind of Jim Crow shanty out of rotten logs—was saving my muscle to cut cord wood.

Next morning bright and early I mounted Satan and rode around hunting some easy trees—ones that I thought would cut nicely. I marked about a dozen and went back to camp, it being noon by that time.

After dinner I lay down to take a nap until evening when it would be cooler. About five o'clock I rolled up my sleeves and waded into a small, sickly pin-oak tree and the way chips flew for half an hour was a caution. I then put in the balance of the evening cording it up—that is what I had cut. It lacked considerable of being half a cord, but I filled in a lot of rotten chunks to make it pan out fifty cents worth. I slept sound that night for I was tired.

Bright and early next morning I shouldered my axe and struck out to tackle another sickly pin-oak tree. While spitting on my hands and figuring on how many licks it would take to down the little sapling, I spied a large coon in a neighboring live-oak. Now catching coons, you all know by this time was a favorite passtime with me, so dropping the axe I went for him. By the time I got part of him cooked it was noon; and after dinner I fell asleep and dreamt happy dreams until after sundown. After supper I went turkey hunting and killed a fat gobbler. Thus ended my third day in a wood camp.

I became tired of the cord wood business after two weeks time. It was too lonesome a work for a boy of my restless disposition. I mounted Satan one morning after devouring the last speck of grub in camp and struck out for the ranch. On my arrival there Mr. Grimes asked me how much wood I had? I told him I thought there was enough to balance my grub bill. He said all right, he would send a man up there with me next morning to measure it. I finally informed him that it wasn't in shape for measuring, with the exception of half a cord that I cut the first day, as it was scattered over a vast territory, two or three sticks in a place.

I suppose he balanced my grub bill as he has never presented it yet.

Just then I came across a factory hand, John Collier by name, who had a boat for sale. He had bought it for a pleasure boat but found he couldn't support such a useless piece of furniture. He offered it to me for forty dollars and he had paid one hundred for it. I tried to sell Satan so as to buy it, but no one would have him as a gift, as they said they would have to get their lives insured before mounting him.

I wanted the boat, but how to get her I did not know. I finally studied up a scheme: Mr. Collier wanted to buy a horse in case he sold the boat, so I began talking horse trade. Nothing but a gentle animal would suit he said. I then described one to him and asked how much he would take to-boot if the pony proved to be as I represented? "Ten dollars" said he; "she pops" continued I. So I started over to Cashe's creek to trade Horace Yeamans out of an old crippled pony that he couldn't get rid of. He was a nice looking horse and apparently as sound as a dollar; but on trotting him around a short while he would become suddenly lame in both of his front legs.

Before starting to Cashe's creek next morning Mr. Collier told me to try and get the horse there that night as, in case we made the trade, he and Mr. Murphy would start next morning on a pleasure trip to Columbia, a town forty miles east. I assured him that I would be back by dark. You see, that was a point gained, making the trade after dark.

I succeeded in making the trade with Horace; he gave me "old gray" as he called him and fourteen dollars in money for my interest in three different brands of cattle. He afterwards sold the cattle for enough to buy a whole herd of crippled ponies.

I rode back to Grimes' ranch very slowly so as not to cause old gray to become lame.

I arrived there about sundown, but remained out in the brush until after dark.

Mr. Collier, on being notified of my arrival, came out, lantern in hand, bringing his friend Murphy along to do the judging for him. He confessed that he was a very poor judge of a spanish pony, not having been long in America. He was from "Hengland."

After examining old gray all over they both pronounced him a model of beauty—an honor to the mustang race. You see, he was hog fat, not having been used for so long.

The trade was sealed that night and next morning Mr. Collier and Murphy, who already had a pony of his own, started on their forty mile journey. When within five miles of Elliott's ferry on the Colorado river, which was fifteen miles from Grimes' old gray gave out entirely, so that poor Collier had to hoof it to the ferry where he secured another horse.

Now kind reader you no doubt think that a shabby trick. If so, all I can say is "such is life in the far west."

Now that I was owner of a ship I concluded it policy to have a partner for company if nothing more, so I persuaded a young factory hand by the name of Sheiseinhamer or some such name to go in with me in my new enterprise. He only had ten dollars to invest, therefore I held the controlling interest.

Our ship was schooner-rigged and would carry about three tons. Her name was "Great Eastern" but we changed it to "The Blood Hound."

I turned Satan loose to rustle for himself (I afterwards sold him to a *stranger* for thirty dollars) and then pulled down the river for Matagorda Bay, a distance of fifteen miles.

I concluded to go to the Peninsula and buy a load of melons that trip, as there were none on Tresspalacious.

We struck the Bay just at dark; the water was terribly rough and the wind was so strong that it made the Blood Hound dip water and slide along as though it was fun. My young pard, who had never been on salt water before, having been raised in Saint Louis, turned pale behind the gills and wanted to turn back when the low streak of land behind us began to grow dim. But as I owned the controlling interest in the ship, I told him he would have to grin and bear it. He swore that would be his last trip and it was. He sold me his interest on the way back for eight dollars; he lost just two dollars besides his time in the speculation.

Finally we hove in sight of the light house at Salura Pass. Then we were all right for I could tell just where to head for, although I hadn't been on the Bay much since leaving there in '67. But I had learned it thoroughly before then.

It was fifteen miles across the Bay to Fred Vogg's landing, where I had concluded to land. We arrived there about midnight and next morning walked up to Mr. Vogg's house, about half a mile, for breakfast. The whole family were glad to see me —for the first time in eight years.

I bought a load of melons delivered at the landing for five cents a head—or piece I should have said.

The next evening we started back home, and arrived at Grimes' just as the whistle was tooting for dinner, next day. The whole crowd of factory hands, there being about seventy-five, made a break for the boat to fill up on melons. The largest I sold at fifty cents and the smallest at twenty-five. By night I had sold entirely out and started back after another load, all by myself this time, with the exception of a dog, a stray that I had picked up.

I bought my melons at a different place this time, from a Mr. Joe Berge who lived a few miles above Mr. Vogg. I got them for two and a half cents a piece, therefore made a better "speck" than before. I struck a terrible storm on my return trip and came very near swamping.

I made my next trip to Indianola as I had four passengers to take down, at two dollars and a half a head.

Shortly after landing in Indianola I got two passengers, one of them a pretty young lady, Miss Ruthie Ward, to take to Sand Point in Lavaca county, just across the Bay from Indianola.

I remained in Indianola two days "bucking" monte. I left there broke after paying for a load of melons.

## 12. BACK TO MY FAVORITE OCCUPATION, THAT OF A WILD AND WOOLLY COW BOY

WHEN the oyster season began, I abandoned the melon trade in favor of the former.

I would load up at one of the many oyster reefs in the Bay and take them either to the factory or Indianola where they sold for one dollar a barrel, in the shell.

Along in October sometime, I worked up a scheme by which I thought I could make a stake. My scheme was to get into the Colorado river where there were no boats and speculate among the africans that lined the river banks on both sides just as far up as it was navigable, which was fifty miles or more.

The worst job was to get the boat into the river, the mouth of it being stopped up with a raft, or "drift" about eighteen miles long.

My only show was to snake her across the prairie from the head of Willson's creek, a distance of five miles—and that I concluded to do if it took all the oxen in Matagorda county.

As I needed a partner in my new enterprise, I managed to find one in the person of an old irishman by the name of "Big

Jack." He only had a capital of eighteen dollars but I agreed to give him half of the profits—which I figured on being very large. You see my intentions were to swap for hides, pecans, etc., which I would have hauled overland to Willson's creek and from there to Indianola by sail boat.

Our plans being laid we struck out for Indianola to buy our goods—all kinds of articles that we thought would catch the negro's eye, including a good supply of tanglefoot—which I am sorry to say cost me dear, besides being the cause of smashing my little scheme into a thousand fragments.

We finally started back from Indianola with our load of goods; and Jack being an irishman, couldn't resist the temptation of taking a "wee drop of the critter" every fifteen or twenty minutes. The consequences were everything but edifying.

I hired Anthony Moore, a gentleman of color to haul the Blood Hound and all of our traps to the river.

We fixed rollers under the boat and after getting her out high and dry on the ball prairie, found that we didn't have oxen enough to carry out the job.

While Anthony Moore was off rustling for a couple more yoke of cattle, I hired a horse to ride up to the Post Office after my mail, but before starting I gave Jack a raking over for remaining drunk so long. He hadn't drawn a sober breath since leaving town.

When I returned next evening Jack was gone—no one there but my faithful dog, Ranger.

I found Jack had taken a negro's skiff and pulled down Willson's creek, taking all of my snide jewelry, tobacco, etc. along. I traced him up to where he had sold a lot of the stuff. He sold an old englishman a lot of tobacco for seven dollars that didn't cost less than twenty. Being discouraged I sold the Blood Hound to Anthony Moore for twenty-five dollars, right where she lay, on the open prairie.

I then hired to Wiley Kuykendall, who was buying and shipping beeves at Houston, at twenty-five dollars per month. I left my companion, Ranger, with Anthony, paying him two dollars and a half a month for his board. But poor dog he met a sad fate the next winter during one of my rash moments.

I was out after a wild bunch of horses one day and while trying to slip up on them unobserved Ranger and three others belonging to a neighbor made a break after a little calf that jumped up out of the tall grass, which of course scared the horses. I wanted to run after them as that was my best and only chance, but I hated to go off and let the dogs kill the poor little calf which they all four had hold of by that time.

I finally galloped back and yelled myself hoarse trying to get them off; but no use, so drawing my pistol I began firing right and left.

When the smoke cleared away I discovered two of the dogs lifeless and poor Ranger crawling up towards me howling with pain. He was shot through both shoulders. No, no! I didn't feel bad; it was some other youngster about my size. I dismounted and caressed the poor dumb brute, with tears in my eyes. It was ten miles to camp or the nearest ranch, therefore I had no alternative but to kill him—or leave him there to suffer and fianlly die. I had tried to lift him on my horse so as to take him to camp and try and doctor him up, but he was too heavy—being a large, powerful brute.

I made several attempts to kill him, but every time I would raise the pistol to shoot he would look up into my eyes so pitifully as much as to say please don't kill me. I at last mounted my horse and after starting off wheeled around in my saddle and put a bullet between his eyes. Thus ended the life of as faithful a dog as ever lived.

After New Year's I quit Mr. Wiley and went to work again on my own hook, skinning cattle and branding Mavricks.

I had bought me a twenty-five dollar horse for the occasion.

I established my camp at the head of Cashe's creek, three miles above Mr. Yeamans.' The only company I had was Ranger and I didn't have him but a short while, as you already know.

Cattle died pretty badly that winter and therefore I made quite a pile of money, besides branding a great many Mavricks.

About the middle of April I met with a painful and almost fatal accident—got shot through the knee with one of those old time dragoon pistols, which carry a very large ball.

The bullet entered the top of my knee and came out—or at least was cut out—on the opposite side; went right through the knee-cap. The doctor who waited on me said I would be a cripple for life, but he missed his guess, although I have received another bullet hole through the same knee since then.

After getting wounded I remained at Mr. Yeamans' awhile and then went down to Mr. Morris' on Tresspalacious Bay to board.

When I got so that I could move around on crutches I went up to Mr. John Pierce's ranch to live. Mr. Pierce had persuaded me to put in my time going to school while unable to work. He gave me my board and washing free and all I had to do was to take care of the "children," little Johnny Pierce, eight years old, Mamie Pierce, "Shang's" only child, twelve years old and a Miss Fannie Elliott, sweet sixteen. The school house being two miles off, we had to ride on horseback.

I would have had a soft time of it all summer, but before two weeks rolled around I had a fuss with the red complexioned school master. I then mounted "Boney-part" and struck out for Houston, ninety miles east.

I arrived in Houston during the State Fair. Everything was lively there—in fact too lively for me. The first thing I did was to strike a monte game and the second thing was to lose nearly all the money I had.

72

After quitting the monte game I struck out to hunt aunt "Mary" whom I heard had moved to Houston from Galveston. I had never seen her that I remembered of, but held her in high esteem for her kindness in sending me the white canvas breeches during the war.

I found her after hunting all day; she kept a private boarding house close to the Union depot. She appeared to be glad to see me.

The next day aunt Mary's husband, Mr. James McClain, took me out to the Fair ground to see the sights. The biggest sight to me was Jeff. Davis, although I was deceived as to his makeup; I expected to see a portly looking man on a gray horse.

May be the following song that I used to sing during the war had something to do with that, for it ran thus:

> *Jeff Davis is our President,*
> *And Lincoln is a fool,*
> *Jeff Davis rides a big gray horse*
> *While Lincoln rides a mule.*

## 13. MOTHER AND I MEET AT LAST

AFTER spending a week with aunt Mary, I grew restless and pulled for Galveston to visit my uncle "Nick." I went by way of steamboat down Buffalo bayou, leaving my horse and saddle in Houston.

I landed in the "Island City" one evening about dark. The first man I met, I inquired of him, if he knew where Mr. Nicholas White lived? "Why of course," was his quick answer, "I have known him for seventeen years." He then gave me the directions how to find him.

His wife, whom he had just married a short while before, she being his second wife, met me at the door and escorted me to the bed room where I found the old fellow three sheets in the wind. He soon braced up though and tendered me a hearty welcome.

The next day he spent in showing me around the city and introducing me to his friends as his little nephew who had to "skip" from western Texas for stealing cattle. I remember there were several high toned officials among the ones he introduced me to; one of them I think was Tom Ochiltree—a red-headed Congressman or Senator, I forget which.

The old gentleman had a horse and buggy, consequently I had a regular picnic, during my stay, driving up and down the beach watching the pretty girls go in bathing.

I remained there two weeks and on taking my departure uncle "Nick" presented me with a Spencer Carbine—one he had captured from a yankee while out scouting during the war. I was very proud of the gift for I had never owned a repeating rifle before.

I landed in Houston flat broke, but wasn't long in making a raise of ten dollars from aunt Mary. Boney-part had been taken good care of during my absence, which made him feel too rollicky—he tried to pitch me off when I got on him.

After bidding aunt Mary and uncle "Jim" good-bye I struck out for Allen, Pool & Co.'s ranch on Simms' bayou. There I hired to a Mr. Joe Davis of Clear creek, who had the contract furnishing beef to the Gulf, Colorado and Santa Fe R. R. which was just building out from Galveston.

About the first of September I mounted Ranger, a pony I swapped Boney-part for and lit out for Tresspalacious. My wound by that time was about well.

On arriving at Mr. "Tom" Kuykendall's at the head of Tresspalacious river, I learned that mother was at Mr. Morris', at the mouth of Cashe's creek, waiting for me. She had arrived there just a few days after my departure—for parts unknown, as no one knew where I was going.

You see after getting shot I wrote to mother telling her of the accident and also sending her some money, as I was in the habit of doing when flush. Hence, like a kind mother, she came out to be of service to me, but arrived too late.

It is needless to say we were glad to meet, for the first time in several long years.

I went right to work trying to rig up a home for her. She had brought some money with her and I sold a lot of Mavricks—

some of those I branded the winter previous—for two dollars a head, therefore we both together had money enough to build and furnish a shanty.

As Mr. Morris was just going to Indianola in his schooner we sent by him after our lumber, etc. But before he got there the "big" storm, which swept nearly every soul from the Peninsula and nearly wiped Indianola out of existence, struck him and scattered his boat, money and everything he had aboard to the four winds of Heaven. He and his son "Tom" barely escaped with their own lives.

Mother and I experienced a share of the same storm too; we were still at Mr. Morris.' The storm came about ten o'clock at night and blew the Morris mansion down, leaving us, Mrs. Morris, her three children and a step-son, "Jim," mother and myself to paddle around in water up to our waists until morning.

When daylight came the Bay shore was lined with dead cattle just as far as the eye could reach; cattle that had blown into the water and drowned.

When Mr. Morris got back he started a new ranch up at the head of Cashe's creek, where I had camped the winter before and I built mother a shanty a few hundred yards from his, so she wouldn't get lonesome while I was away.

I built it out of an old torn down house that I bought from Mr. John Pierce on "tick" for I was then financially "busted."

Cattle didn't die very badly that coming winter, therefore I did not make much money. But towards spring I got my work in branding Mavricks. Some days I would brand as high as fifteen or twenty head.

That spring there was a law passed prohibiting the carrying of pistols and I was the first man to break the law, for which they socked a heavier fine to me than I was able to pay; but I found a good friend in the person of Mr. John Pierce who loaned me the desired amount without asking for it.

The first of April I hired to W. B. Grimes to go "up the

trail" at thirty dollars per month. I bade mother good bye, promising to return, sure, that coming fall.

Our outfit consisted of twenty-five hundred head of old mossy-horn steers, a cook and twenty-five riders, including the boss, Asa Dawdy, with six head of good horses to the man.

Everything went on lovely with the exception of swimming swollen streams, fighting now and then among ourselves and a stampede every stormy night, until we arrived on the Canadian river in the Indian territory; there we had a little indian scare. When within a few miles of the river, Dawdy went on ahead to look up a good crossing; it wasn't long until we discovered a terrible dust on the trail between us and the river; it looked like it might be a cyclone coming, but instead of that it was our boss returning. He galloped up almost out of wind telling us to stop the herd and make preparations for war, as the woods along the river were covered with indians on the war path.

After getting everything in shape for war, he selected two of his best armed men, which happened to be Otto Draub and myself, to go back with him and try to make peace with the red devils. We scoured the woods out thoroughly, but only succeeded in finding one old, blind "buck." Asa had, no doubt, seen him and imagined the rest. From that time on though we were among indians all the time; and they used to try and scare Asa into giving them "wo-ha's," (cattle) but he wasn't one of the scaring kind—except when taken by surprise.

Everything went on smoothly again until we arrived at "Salt Fork" close to the Kansas line. It was raining and storming terribly when we hove in sight of the above named river. Asa went on ahead with the wagons—we having an extra one along then to haul wood and water in—to find a crossing, but on arriving there he found it very high, almost swimming; he succeeded in getting both wagons over though. He then galloped back to hurry the herd up.

We were just about a mile from the river when he came dashing up saying: "Whoop 'em up boys! for she's rising a foot every second."

When we got there she was "bank full" and still rising. It was at least half a mile to the opposite side and drift wood was coming down at a terrible rate, which made it dangerous to cross. But the wagons being over made it a ground hog case —or at least we thought so.

The old lead steers went right into the foaming water without a bit of trouble and of course the balance followed.

Henry Coats was in the lead of the herd, Asa Dawdy and Otto Draub on the left point, while negro "Gabe" and I kept them from turning to the right.

We were all—that is we fellows on the points—out in swimming water when Henry Coats' horse went under, which scared the leaders, causing the whole herd to turn back amidst terrible confusion. Coats came very near drowning. We worked for half an hour or more trying to get the herd to take water again, but failed. The river continued to rise until she was over a mile wide.

Suffice it to say, we remained there seven days without anything to eat except fresh meat without salt. It rained during the whole time nearly, so that we didn't get much sleep on account of having to stay with the cattle night and day.

The first grub we got was from a lot of soldiers camped on the opposite side of the wicked little stream "Wild Horse." They were waiting for it to go down so they could proceed to Wichita, Kansas, their destination.

The boss, Dawdy, a fellow by the name of Hastings and myself found the "blue coats" while out hunting a lot of steers lost the night before during a severe storm. We had spied the white tents off to the southward and pulled out for them, in a gallop.

On arriving within a few hundred yards we found out that a swift stream of muddy water laid between us.

They were camped right on the opposite bank from where we stood. Dawdy yelled over asking if they could spare some chuck? "Yes" was the quick response, "If you will come over after it."

Dawdy and Hastings both looked at me, as much as to say: "Charlie it all depends on you." I was considered an extra good swimmer.

After shedding my heaviest clothes—there being officers' wives in camp, so that I couldn't undress altogether—I put spurs to "Yankee-doodle" and went into her. It was at least two hundred yards across, but I made it all O. K.

When the captain found out how long we had been without grub he ordered the cook to bring out some cold biscuits. He brought out a large pan full, and after I got my fists full, a lot of the soldiers took the balance and selecting a narrow place, threw them over one by one to Dawdy and Hastings.

After hiding a dozen or two fat Government biscuits under my belt, I began studying up a plan by which I could get some flour and salt, also coffee, over. At last I hit upon a plan: I got a wash-tub from the captain's wife and filling it full of such stuff as we needed, launched her out into the water; I swam by the side of it and landed on the opposite side about half a mile below where I started in at. I then took the tub back, thanked our benefactors, mounted Yankee-doodle and pulled for the other shore feeling a thousand per cent. better.

We arrived at camp about sundown and the boys went to work baking bread by rolling the dough around a stick and holding it over the fire. Some of them sat up all night eating, trying to make up for lost time.

The sun came out next morning for the first time in eight long days and towards evening we made it across the river. The wagons we found at the "Pond Creek" ranch on the Kansas line. The cooks had been having a soft time.

## 14. ON A TARE IN WICHITA, KANSAS

O<small>N THE</small> fourth day of July, after being on the trail just three months, we landed on the "Ninnasquaw" river, thirty miles west of Wichita, Kansas.

Nearly all the boys, the boss included, struck out for Wichita right away to take the train for Houston, Texas, the nearest railroad point to their respective homes. Mr. Grimes paid their railroad fares according to custom in those days. I concluded I would remain until fall.

Mr. Grimes had come around by rail, consequently he was on hand to receive us. He already had several thousand steers—besides our herd—on hand; some that he drove up the year before and others he bought around there. He had them divided up into several different herds—about eight hundred to the herd—and scattered out into different places, that is each camp off by itself, from five to ten miles from any other. With each herd or bunch would be a cook and "chuck" wagon, four riders, a "boss" included—and five horses to the rider. During the day two men would "herd" or watch the cattle until noon and the other two until time to "bed" them, which would be about dark. By "bedding" we mean take them to camp, to a certain high piece of ground suitable for a "bed ground" where they would all lie down until morning, unless disturbed by a storm or otherwise. The nights would be divided up into four equal parts—one man "on" at a time, unless storming, tormented with mosquitos or something of the kind, when every one except the cook would have to be "out" singing to them.

The herd I came up the trail with was split into three bunches and I was put with one of them under a man by the name of Phillups, but shortly afterwards changed and put with a Mr. Taylor.

I spent all my extra time when not on duty, visiting a couple of New York damsels, who lived with their parents five miles east of our camp. They were the only young ladies in the neighborhood, the country being very thinly settled then, therefore the boys thought I was very "cheeky"—getting on courting terms with them so quick. One of them finally "put a head on me"—or in grammatical words, gave me a black eye—which chopped my visits short off; she didn't understand the Texas way of proposing for one's hand in marriage, was what caused the fracas. She was cleaning roasting-ears for dinner when I asked her how she would like to jump into double harness and trot through life with me? The air was full of flying roasting-ears for a few seconds—one of them striking me over the left eye—and shortly afterwards a young Cow Puncher rode into camp with one eye in a sling. You can imagine the boys giving it to me about monkeying with civilized girls, etc.

After that I became very lonesome; had nothing to think of but my little Texas girl—the only one on earth I loved. While sitting "on herd" in the hot sun, or lounging around camp in the shade of the wagon—there being no trees in that country to supply us with shade—my mind would be on nothing but her. I finally concluded to write to her and find out just how I stood. As often as I had been with her I had never let her know

81

my thoughts. She being only fourteen years of age, I thought there was plenty time. I wrote a long letter explaining everything and then waited patiently for an answer. I felt sure she would give me encouragement, if nothing more.

A month passed by and still no answer. Can it be possible that she don't think enough of me to answer my letter? thought I. "No," I would finally decide, "she is too much of an angel to be guilty of such."

At last the supply wagon arrived from Wichita and among the mail was a letter for me. I was on herd that forenoon and when the other boys came out to relieve Collier and I, they told me about there being a letter in camp for me, written by a female, judging from the fine hand-writing on the envelope.

I was happy until I opened the letter and read a few lines. It then dropped from my fingers and I turned deathly pale. Mr. Collier wanted to know if some of my relations wasn't dead? Suffice it to say that the object of my heart was married to my old playmate Billy Williams. The letter went on to state that she had given her love to another and that she never thought I loved her only as a friend, etc. She furthermore went on advising me to grin and bear it, as there were just as good fish in the sea as ever was caught etc.

I wanted some one to kill me, so concluded to go to the Black hills—as everyone was flocking there then. Mr. Collier, the same man I traded the crippled horse to—agreed to go with me. So we both struck out for Wichita to settle up with daddy Grimes. Mr. Collier had a good horse of his own and so did I; mine was a California pony that I had given fifty-five dollars for quite awhile before. My intention was to take him home and make a race horse of him; he was only three years old and according to my views a "lightning striker."

After settling up, we, like other "locoed" Cow Punchers proceeded to take in the town, and the result was, after two or three days carousing around, we left there "busted" with the exception of a few dollars.

As we didn't have money enough to take us to the Black hills, we concluded to pull for the Medicine river, one hundred miles west.

We arrived in Kiowa, a little one-horse town on the Medicine, about dark one cold and disagreeable evening.

We put up at the Davis House, which was kept by a man named Davis—by the way one of the whitest men that ever wore shoes. Collier made arrangements that night with Mr. Davis to board us on "tick" until we could get work. But I wouldn't agree to that.

The next morning after paying my night's lodging I had just one dollar left and I gave that to Mr. Collier as I bade him adieu. I then headed southwest across the hills, not having any destination in view; I wanted to go somewhere but didn't care where. To tell the truth I was still somewhat rattled over my recent bad luck.

That night I lay out in the brush by myself and next morning changed my course to southeast, down a creek called Driftwood. About noon I accidentally landed in Gus Johnson's Cow camp at the forks of Driftwood and "Little Mule" creeks.

I remained there all night and next morning when I was fixing to pull out—God only knows where, the boss, Bill Hudson, asked me if I wouldn't stay and work in his place until he went to Hutchison, Kansas and back? I agreed to do so finally if he would furnish "Whisky-peat," my pony, all the corn he could eat—over and above my wages, which were to be twenty-five dollars a month. The outfit consisted of only about twenty-five hundred Texas steers, a chuck wagon, cook and five riders besides the boss.

A few days after Mr. Hudson left we experienced a terrible severe snow storm. We had to stay with the drifting herd night

83

and day, therefore it went rough with us—myself especially, being from a warm climate and only clad in common garments, while the other boys were fixed for winter.

When Mr. Hudson came back from Hutchison he pulled up stakes and drifted south down into the Indian territory—our camp was then on the territory and Kansas line—in search of good winter quarters.

We located on the "Eagle Chief" river, a place where cattle had never been held before. Cattlemen in that section of country considered it better policy to hug the Kansas line on account of indians.

About the time we became settled in our new quarters, my month was up and Mr. Hudson paid me twenty-five dollars, telling me to make that my home all winter if I wished.

My "pile" now amounted to forty-five dollars, having won twenty dollars from one of the boys, Ike Berry, on a horse race. They had a race horse in camp called "Gray-dog," who had never been beaten, so they said, but I and Whisky-peat done him up, to the extent of twenty dollars, in fine shape.

I made up my mind that I would build me a "dugout" somewhere close to the Johnson camp and put in the winter hunting and trapping. Therefore as Hudson was going to Kiowa, with the wagon, after a load of provisions, etc., I went along to lay me in a supply also.

On arriving at Kiowa I found that my old "pard" Mr. Collier had struck a job with a cattleman whose ranch was close to town. But before spring he left for good "Hold Hengland" where a large pile of money was awaiting him; one of his rich relations had died and willed him everything he had. We suppose he is now putting on lots of "agony," if not dead, and telling his green countrymen of his hair-breadth escapes on the wild Texas plains.

We often wonder if he forgets to tell of his experience with "old gray," the pony I traded to him for the boat.

After sending mother twenty dollars by registered mail and laying in a supply of corn, provisions, ammunition, etc., I pulled back to Eagle Chief, to make war with wild animals—especially those that their hides would bring me in some money, such as gray wolves, coyotes, wild cats, buffaloes and bears. I left Kiowa with just three dollars in money.

The next morning after arriving in camp I took my stuff and moved down the river about a mile to where I had already selected a spot for my winter quarters.

I worked like a turk all day long building me a house out of dry poles—covered with grass. In the north end I built a "sod" chimney and in the south end, left an opening for a door. When finished it lacked about two feet of being high enough for me to stand up straight.

It was almost dark and snowing terribly when I got it finished and a fire burning in the low, Jim Crow fire-place. I then fed Whisky-peat some corn and stepped out a few yards after an armful of good solid wood for morning. On getting about half an armful of wood gathered I heard something crackling and looking over my shoulder discovered my mansion in flames. I got there in time to save nearly everything in the shape of bedding, etc. Some of the grub, being next to the fire-place, was lost. I slept at Johnson's camp that night.

The next morning I went about two miles down the river and located another camp. This time I built a dug-out right on the bank of the stream, in a thick bunch of timber.

I made the dug-out in a curious shape; started in at the edge of the steep bank and dug a place six feet long, three deep and three wide, leaving the end next to the creek open for a door. I then commenced at the further end and dug another place same size in an opposite direction, which formed an "L." I then dug still another place, same size, straight out from the river which made the whole concern almost in the shape of a "Z." In the end furthest from the stream I made a fire-place by digging the earth away—in the shape of a regular fire-place. And then to make a chimney I dug a round hole, with the aid of a butcher knife, straight up as far as I could reach; then commencing at the top and connecting the two holes. The next thing was to make it "draw," and I did that by cutting and piling sods of dirt around the hole, until about two feet above the level.

I then proceeded to build a roof over my 3 x 18 mansion. To do that I cut green poles four feet long and laid them across the top, two or three inches apart. Then a layer of grass and finally, to finish it off, a foot of solid earth. She was then ready for business. My idea in making it so crooked was, to keep the indians, should any happen along at night, from seeing my fire. After getting established in my new quarters I put out quite a number of wolf baits and next morning in going to look at them found several dead wolves besides scores of skunks, etc. But they were frozen too stiff to skin, therefore I left them until a warmer day.

The next morning on crawling out to feed my horse I discovered it snowing terribly, accompanied with a piercing cold norther. I crawled back into my hole after making Whisky-peat as comfortable as possible and remained there until late in the evening, when suddenly disturbed by a horny visitor.

It was three or four o'clock in the evening, while humped up before a blazing fire, thinking of days gone by, that all at once, before I had time to think, a large red steer came tumbling down head first, just missing me by a few inches. In traveling ahead of the storm the whole Johnson herd had passed right over me, but luckily only one broke through.

86

Talk about your ticklish places! That was truly one of them; a steer jammed in between me and daylight, and a hot fire roasting me by inches.

I tried to get up through the roof—it being only a foot above my head—but failed. Finally the old steer made a terrible struggle, just about the time I was fixing to turn my wicked soul over to the Lord, and I got a glimpse of daylight under his flanks. I made a dive for it and by tight squeezing I saved my life.

After getting out and shaking myself I made a vow that I would leave that God-forsaken country in less than twenty-four hours; and I did so.

## 15. A LONELY TRIP DOWN THE CIMERON

THE next morning after the steer racket I pulled out for Kiowa, Kansas. It was then sleeting from the north, consequently I had to face it.

About three oclock in the evening I changed my notion and concluded to head for Texas. So I turned east, down the Eagle Chief, to where it emptied into the Cimeron, and thence down that stream; knowing that I was bound to strike the Chisholm trail—the one I came up on, the spring before.

I camped that night at the mouth of Eagle Chief and went to roost on an empty stomach, not having brought any grub with me. I was then in the western edge of what is known as the Blawk-jack country, which extends east far beyond the Chisholm trail.

The next morning I continued down the Cimeron, through Black-jack timber and sand hills. To avoid the sand hills, which appeared fewer on the opposite side, I undertook to cross the river, but bogged down in the quicksand and had to turn back.

That night I camped between two large sand hills and made my bed in a tall bunch of blue-stem grass. I went to bed as full as a tick, as I had just eaten a mule-eared rabbit, one I had slipped up onto and killed with a club. I was afraid to shoot at the large droves of deer and turkeys, on account of the country being full of fresh indian signs.

I crawled out of my nest next morning almost frozen. I built a roaring big fire on the *south* edge of the bunch of tall grass so as to check the cold piercing norther. After enjoying the warm fire a few moments, I began to get thirsty and there being no water near at hand, I took my tin cup and walked over to a large snow-drift a short distance off, to get it full of clean snow, which I intended melting by the fire to quench my burning thirst.

While filling the cup I heard a crackling noise behind me and looking over my shoulder discovered a blaze of fire twenty feet in the air and spreading at a terrible rate. I arrived on the scene just in time to save Whisky-peat from a horrible death. He was tied to a tree, the top limbs of which were already in a blaze. I also managed to save my saddle and an old piece of saddle blanket, they being out under the tree that Whisky-peat was tied to. I didn't mind losing my leather leggins, saddle blankets, etc., so much as I did the old delapidated overcoat that contained a little silver-plated match box in one of the pockets.

That day I traveled steady, but not making very rapid progress, on account of winding around sand hills, watching for indians and going around the heads of boggy sloughs. I was certain of striking the Chisholm trail before night, but was doomed to disappointment.

I pitched camp about nine o'clock that night and played a single-handed game of freeze-out until morning, not having any matches to make a fire with.

I hadn't gone more than two miles next morning when I came across a camp-fire, which looked as though it had been used a few hours before; on examination I found it had been an indian camp, just vacated that morning. The trail, which contained the tracks of forty or fifty head of horses, led down the river. After warming myself I struck right out on their trail, being very cautious not to run onto them. Every now and then I would dismount and crawl to the top of a tall sand hill to see that the road was clear ahead.

About noon I came to a large creek, which proved to be "Turkey Creek." The reds had made a good crossing by digging the banks down and breaking the ice.

After crossing, I hadn't gone but a short distance when I came in sight of the Chisholm trail. I never was so glad to see anything before—unless it was the little streak of daylight under the steer's flanks.

The indians on striking the trail had struck south on it; and after crossing the Cimeron I came in sight of them, about five miles ahead of me. I rode slow so as to let them get out of sight. I didn't care to come in contact with them for fear they might want my horse and possibly my scalp.

About dark that evening I rode into a large camp of Government freighters, who informed me that the fifty indians who had just passed—being on their way back to the reservation— were Kiowas who had been on a hunting expedition.

I fared well that night, got a good supper and a warm bed to sleep in—besides a good square meal of corn and oats for my horse.

The next morning before starting on my journey, an old irish teamster by the name of "Long Mike" presented me with a pair of pants—mine being almost in rags—and a blue soldier coat, which I can assure you I appreciated very much.

About dusk that evening, I rode into Cheyenne Agency and that night slept in a house for the first time since leaving Kiowa —in fact I hadn't seen a house since leaving Kiowa.

The next morning I continued south and that night put up at "Bill" Williams' ranch on the "South Canadian" river.

Shortly after leaving the Williams ranch next morning I met a crowd of Chickasaw indians who bantered me for a horse race. As Whisky-peat was tired and foot-sore, I refused; but they kept after me until finally I took them up. I put up my saddle and pistol against one of their ponies. The pistol I kept buckled around me for fear they might try to swindle me. The saddle I put up and rode the race bare-back. I came out ahead, but not enough to brag about. They gave up the pony without a murmer, but tried to persuade me to run against one of their other ponies, a much larger and finer looking one. I rode off thanking them very kindly for what they had already done for me.

That night I put up at a ranch on the Washita river and next morning before leaving swapped my indian pony off for another one and got ten dollars to-boot.

That morning I left the Chisholm trail and struck down the Washita river, in search of a good, lively place where I might put in the balance of the winter.

I landed in Erin Springs late that evening and found a grand ball in full bloom at Frank Murry's mansion. The dancers were a mixed crowd, the ladies being half-breeds and the men, mostly americans and very tough citizens.

Of course I joined the mob, being in search of excitement and had a gay old time drinking kill-me-quick whisky and swinging the pretty indian maidens.

After breakfast next morning the whole crowd, ladies and all, went down the river five miles to witness a "big" horse race at "Kickapoo" flat.

After the "big" race—which was for several thousand dollars —was over the day was spent in running pony races and drinking whisky. By night the whole mob were gloriously drunk, your humble servant included. There were several fights and fusses took place during the day, but no one seriously hurt.

It being against the laws of the United States to sell, or have whisky in the Indian territory, you might wonder where it came from: A man by the name of Bill Anderson—said to have been one of Quantrell's men during the war—did the selling.

He defied the United States marshalls and it was said that he had over a hundred indictments against him. He sold it at ten dollars a gallon, therefore you see he could afford to run quite a risk.

The next day on my way down the river to Paul's valley I got rid of my extra pony; I came across two apple peddlers who were on their way to Fort Sill with a load of apples and who had had the misfortune of losing one of their horses by death, the night before, thereby leaving them on the prairie helpless, unable to move on. They had no money to buy another horse with, having spent all their surplus wealth in Arkansas for the load of apples. When I gave them the pony, they felt very happy, judging from their actions. On taking my departure one of them insisted on my taking his silver watch as a token of friendship. I afterwards had the watch stolen from me.

Well, patient reader, I will now drop the curtain for awhile. Just suffice it to say I had a tough time of it during the rest of the winter and came out carrying two bullet wounds. But I had some gay times as well as tough and won considerable money running Whisky-peat.

The following May I landed in Gainesville, Texas, "right side up with care" and from there went to Saint Joe on the Chisholm trail, where I succeeded in getting a job with a passing herd belonging to Capt. Littlefield of Gonzales. The boss' name was "Jim" Wells and the herd contained thirty-five hundred head of stock cattle. It being a terribly wet season we experienced considerable hardships, swimming swollen streams, etc. We also had some trouble with indians.

We arrived in Dodge City, Kansas on the third day of July and that night I quit and went to town to "whoop 'em up Liza Jane."

I met an old friend that night by the name of "Wess" Adams and we both had a gay time, until towards morning when he got severely stabbed in a free-to-all fight.

On the morning of July fifth I hired to David T. Beals—or the firm of Bates & Beals, as the outfit was commonly called—to help drive a herd of steers, twenty-five hundred head, to the Panhandle of Texas, where he intended starting a new ranch.

The next morning we struck out on the "Old Fort Bascom" trail, in a southwesterly direction.

The outfit consisted of eight men besides the boss, Bill Allen and "Deacon" Bates, one of Mr. Beals' silent partners, who was going along to locate the new range and O. M. Johnson, the whole-souled ex-rebel cook. We had six extra good horses apiece, my six being named as follows: Comanche, Allisan, Last Chance, Creeping Moses, Damfido and Beat-and-be-damned. The last named was afterwards shot full of arrows because he wouldn't hurry while being driven off by a band of indians who had made a raid on the camp.

# 16. MY FIRST EXPERIENCE ROPING A BUFFALO

ABOUT the sixth day out from Dodge we crossed the Cimeron and that evening I had a little excitement chasing a herd of buffaloes.

After crossing the river about noon, we drove out to the divide, five or six miles and made a "dry" camp. It was my evening to lay in camp, or do anything else I wished. Therefore concluded I would saddle my little indian mare—one I had traded for from an indian—and take a hunt.

About the time I was nearly ready to go Mr. Bates, seeing some of the cattle slipping off into a bunch of sand hills which were near the herd, asked me if I wouldn't ride out and turn them back. I went, leaving my pistol and gun in camp, thinking of course that I would be back in a few minutes. But instead of that I didn't get back until after dinner the next day.

Just as I was starting back to camp, after turning the cattle, a large herd of buffaloes dashed by camp headed west. The boys all ran out with their guns and began firing. I became excited and putting spurs to my pony, struck out to overtake and kill a few of them, forgetting that I didn't have anything to shoot with. As they had over a mile the start it wasn't an easy matter to overtake them. It was about four o'clock in the afternoon and terribly hot; which of course cut off my pony's wind and checked her speed to a great extent.

About sundown I overtook them. Their tongues were sticking out a yard. I took down my rope from the saddle-horn, having just missed my shooting irons a few minutes before, and threw it onto a yearling heifer. When the rope tightened the yearling began to bleat and its mammy broke back out of the herd and took after me. I tried to turn the rope loose so as to get out of the way, but couldn't, as it was drawn very tight around the saddle-horn. To my great delight, after raking some of the surplus hair from my pony's hind quarters, she turned and struck out after the still fleeing herd.

Now the question arose in my mind, "how are you going to kill your buffalo?" Break her neck was the only way I could thing of; after trying it several times by running "against" the rope at full speed, I gave it up as a failure. I then concluded to cut the rope and let her go, so getting out my old frog-sticker—an old pocket knife I had picked up a few days before and which I used to clean my pipe—I went to work trying to open the little blade it being the only one that would cut hot butter. The big blade was open when I found it, consequently it was nothing but a sheet of rust. The little blade had become rusted considerably, which made it hard to open. Previous to that I always used my bowie knife, which at that time was hanging to my pistol belt, in camp, to open it with. After working a few minutes I gave up the notion of opening the little blade and went to work sawing at the rope with the big one. But I soon gave that up also, as I could have made just as much headway by cutting with my finger. At last I dismounted and went to him, or at least her, with nothing but my muscle for a weapon.

I finally managed to get her down by getting one hand fastened to her under jaw and the other hold of one horn and then twisting her neck. As some of you might wonder why I had so much trouble with this little animal, when it is a known fact that one man by himself can tie down the largest domestic bull that ever lived, I will say that the difference between a buffalo and a domestic bull is, that the latter when you throw him hard against the ground two or three times, will lie still long enough to give you a chance to jump aboard of him, while the former will raise to his feet, instantly, just as long as there's a bit of life left.

After getting her tied down with my "sash," a silk concern that I kept my breeches up with, I went to work opening the little blade of my knife. I broke the big one off and then used it for a pry to open the other with.

When I got her throat cut I concluded it a good idea to take the hide along, to show the boys that I didn't have my run for nothing, so went to work skinning, which I found to be a tedious job with such a small knife-blade.

It was pitch dark when I started towards camp with the hide and a small chunk of meat tied behind my saddle.

After riding east about a mile, I abandoned the idea of going to camp and turned south facing the cool breeze in hopes of finding water, my pony and I both being nearly dead for a drink.

It was at least twenty miles to camp over a level, dry plain, therefore I imagined it an impossibility to go that distance without water. As the streams all lay east and west in that country, I knew by going south I was bound to strike one sooner or later.

About midnight I began to get sleepy, so, pulling the bridle off my pony so she could graze, I spread the buffalo hide down, hair up, and after wrapping the end of the rope, that my pony was fastened to around my body once or twice so she couldn't get loose without me knowing it, fell asleep.

I hadn't slept long when I awoke, covered from head to foot with ants. The fresh hide had attracted them.

After freeing myself of most of the little pests, I continued my journey in search of water.

About three o'clock in the morning I lay down again, but this time left the hide on my saddle.

I think I must have been asleep about an hour when all at once my pony gave a tremendous snort and struck out at full speed, dragging me after her.

You see I had wrapped the rope around my body as before and it held me fast some way or another; I suppose by getting tangled. Luckily for me though it came loose after dragging me about a hundred yards.

You can imagine my feelings on gaining my feet, and finding myself standing on the broad prairie afoot. I felt just like a little boy does when he lets a bird slip out of his hand accidenty —that is—exceedingly foolish.

The earth was still shaking and I could hear a roaring noise like that of distant thunder. A large herd of buffaloes had just passed.

While standing scratching my head a faint noise greeted my ear; it was my pony snorting. A tramp of about three hundred yards brought me to her. She was shaking as though she had a chill. I mounted and continued my journey south, determined on not stopping any more that night.

About ten o'clock next morning I struck water on the head of Sharp's creek, a tributary to "Beaver" or head of North Canadian.

When I got to camp—it having been moved south about twenty miles from where I left it—the boys had just eaten dinner and two of them were fixing to go back and hunt me up, thinking some sad misfortune had befallen me.

When we got to Blue Creek, a tributary to South Canadian, camp was located for awhile, until a suitable location could be found for a permanent ranch.

Mr. Bates struck out across the country to the Canadian river, taking me along, to hunt the range—one large enough for at least fifty thousand cattle.

After being out three days we landed in Tascosa, a little mexican town on the Canadian. There were only two americans there, Howard & Reinheart, who kept the only store in town. Their stock of goods consisted of three barrels of whisky and half a dozen boxes of soda crackers.

From there we went down the river twenty-five miles where we found a little trading point, consisting of one store and two mexican families. The store, which was kept by a man named Pitcher, had nothing in it but whisky and tobacco. His customers were mostly transient buffalo hunters, they being mostly indians and mexicans. He also made a business of dealing in robes, furs, etc., which he shipped to Fort Lyons, Colorado, where his partner, an officer in the United States Army lived. There were three hundred Apache indians camped right across the river from "Cold Springs," as Pitcher called his ranch.

A few miles below where the little store stood Mr. Bates decided on being the center of the "L. X." range; and right there, Wheeler post-office now stands. And that same range, which was then black with buffaloes, is now stocked with seventy-five thousand fine blooded cattle, and all fenced in. So you see time makes changes, even out here in the "western wilds."

# 17. AN EXCITING TRIP AFTER THIEVES

AFTER arriving on our newly located ranch we counted the cattle and found the herd three hundred head short.

Bill Allen, the boss, struck back to try and find their trail. He found it leading south from the "rifle pits." The cattle had stolen out of the herd without anyone finding it out; and of course finding themselves free, they having come from southern Texas, they headed south across the Plains.

Allen came back to camp and taking me and two horses apiece, struck down the river to head them off. We made our headquarters at Fort Elliott and scoured the country out for a hundred miles square.

We succeeded in getting about two hundred head of them; some had become wild and were mixed up with large herds of buffalo, while others had been taken up by ranchmen around the Fort and the brands disfigured. We got back to camp after being absent a month.

About the first of October four more herds arrived; three from Dodge and one from Grenada, Colorado, where Bates & Beals formerly had a large ranch. We then turned them all loose on the river and established "Sign" camps around the entire range, which was about forty miles square. The camps were stationed from twenty-five to thirty miles apart. There were two men to the camp and their duty was to see that no cattle drifted outside of the line—on their "ride," which was half way to the next camp on each side, or in plainer words one man would ride south towards the camp in that direction, while his pard would go north until he met the man from the next camp, which would generally be on a hill, as near half way as possible. If any cattle had crossed over the line during the night they would leave a trail of course, and this the rider would follow up until he overtook them. He would then bring them back inside of the line; sometimes though they would come out so thick that half a dozen men couldn't keep them back, for instance, during a bad storm. Under such circumstances he would have to do the best he could until he got a chance to send to the "home ranch" for help.

A young man by the name of John Robinson and myself were put in a Sign camp ten miles south of the river, at the foot of the Staked Plains. It was the worst camp in the whole business, for three different reasons, the first one being, cattle naturally want to drift south in the winter, and secondly, the cold storms always came from the north, and the third and most objection-able cause was, if any happened to get over the line onto the Staked plains during a bad snow storm they were considered gone, as there were no "breaks" or anything to check them for quite a distance. For instance, drifting southwest they would have nothing but a level plain to travel over for a distance of three hundred miles to the Pecos river near the old Mexico line.

John and I built a small stone house on the head of "Bonetta" Canyon and had a hog killing time all by ourselves. Hunting was our delight at first, until it became old. We always had four or five different kinds of meat in camp. Buffalo meat was way below par with us, for we could go a few hundred yards from camp any time of day and kill any number of the woolly brutes. To give you an idea how thick buffaloes were around there that fall will say, at one time when we first located our camp on the Bonetta, there was a solid string of them, from one to three miles wide, going south, which took three days and nights to cross the Canadian river. And at other times I have seen them so thick on the plains that the country would look black just as far as the eye could reach.

Late that fall we had a change in bosses. Mr. Allen went home to Corpus Christi, Texas, and a man by the name of Moore came down from Colorado and took his place.

About Christmas we had a little excitement, chasing some mexican thieves, who robbed Mr. Pitcher of everything he had in his little Jim Crow store. John and I were absent from our camp, six days on this trip. There were nine of us in the persuing party, headed by Mr. Moore, our boss. We caught the outfit, which consisted of five men, all well armed and three women, two of them being pretty maidens, on the staked plains, headed for Mexico. It was on this trip that I swore off getting drunk, and I have stuck to it—with the exception of once and that was over the election of President Cleveland—It happened thus:

We rode into Tascosa about an hour after dark, having been in the saddle and on a hot trail all day without food or water. Supper being ordered we passed off the time waiting, by sampling Howard and Reinheart's bug juice.

Supper was called and the boys all rushed to the table—a few sheepskins spread on the dirt floor. When about through they missed one of their crowd—a fellow about my size. On searching far and near he was found lying helplessly drunk under his horse, Whisky-peet—who was tied to a rack in front of the store. A few glasses of salty water administered by Mr. Moore brought me to my right mind. Moore then after advising me to remain until morning, not being able to endure an all night ride as he thought, called, "come on, fellers!" And mounting their tired horses they dashed off at almost full speed.

There I stood leaning against the rack not feeling able to move. Whisky-peet was rearing and prancing in his great anxiety to follow the crowd. I finally climbed into the saddle, the pony still tied to the rack. I had sense enough left to know that I couldn't get on him if loose, in the fix I was in. Then pulling out my bowie knife I cut the rope and hugged the saddle-horn with both hands. I overtook and stayed with the crowd all night, but if ever a mortal suffered it was me. My stomach felt as though it was filled with scorpions, wild cats and lizards. I swore if God would forgive me for geting on that drunk I would never do so again. But the promise was broken, as I stated before, when I received the glorious news of Cleveland's election.

After New Year's, Moore took Jack Ryan, Vandozen and myself and went on an exploring expedition south, across the Staked plains, with a view of learning the country.

The first place we struck was Canyon Paladuro, head of Red river. The whole country over there was full of indians and mexicans. We laid over two days in one of their camps, watching them lance buffaloes. From there we went to Mulberry where we put in three or four days hunting. When we pulled out again our pack-pony was loaded down with fat bear meat.

## 18. SEVEN WEEKS AMONG INDIANS

O<small>N OUR</small> arrival back to the ranch, Moore rigged up a scouting outfit to do nothing but drift over the Plains in search of strayed cattle.

The outfit consisted of a well-filled chuck-wagon, a number one good cook, Mr. O. M. Johnson, and three warriors, Jack Ryan, Vanduzen and myself. We had two good horses apiece, that is, all but myself, I had three counting Whisky-peet.

About the sixth day out we struck three thousand Comanche Indians and became pretty badly scared up. We had camped for the night on the plains, at the forks of Mulberry and Canyon Paladuro; a point from whence could be seen one of the roughest and most picturesque scopes of country in the west.

The next morning Jack Ryan went with the wagon to pilot it across Mulberry Canyon, while "Van" and I branched off down into Canyon Paladuro to look for cattle signs. We succeeded in finding two little knotty-headed two-year old steers with a bunch of buffalo. They were almost as wild as their woolly associates, but we managed to get them cut out and headed in the direction the wagon had gone.

About noon, on turning a sharp curve in the canyon, we suddenly came in full view of our wagon surrounded with a couple of thousand red skins, on horse back, and others still pouring down from the hills, on the east.

It was too late to figure on what to do, for they had already seen us, only being about half a mile off. You see the two wild steers had turned the curve ahead of us and attracted the indians attention in that direction. We couldn't see anything but the white top of our wagon, on account of the solid mass of reds, hence couldn't tell whether our boys were still among the living or not. We thought of running once, but finally concluded to go up and take our medicine like little men, in case they were on the war-path. Leaving Whisky-peet, who was tied behind the wagon, kept me from running more than anything else.

On pushing our way through the mass we found the boys, winchesters in hand, telling the old chiefs where to find plenty of buffalo. There were three thousand in the band, and they had just come from Ft. Sill, Indian Territory, on a hunting expedition. They wanted to get where buffaloes were plentiful before locating winter quarters.

From that time on we were among indians all the time. The Pawnee tribe was the next we came in contact with. Close to the Indian Territory line we run afoul of the whole Cheyenne tribe. They were half starved, all the buffalo having drifted south, and their ponies being too poor and weak to follow them up. We traded them out of lots of blankets, trinkets, etc. For a pint of flour or coffee they would give their whole soul—and body thrown in for good measure. We soon ran out of chuck too, having swapped it all off to the hungry devils.

We then circled around by Ft. Elliott, and up the Canadian river to the ranch, arriving there with eighteen head of our steers, after an absence of seven weeks.

We only got to remain at the ranch long enough to get a new supply of chuck, etc., and a fresh lot of horses, as Moore sent us right back to the Plains. In a south-westerly direction this time.

We remained on the Plains scouting around during the rest of the winter, only making short trips to the ranch after fresh horses and grub. We experienced some tough times too, especially during severe snow storms when our only fuel, "buffalo-chips," would be covered up in the deep snow. Even after the snow melted off, for several days afterwards, we couldn't get much warmth out of the buffalo-chips, on account of them being wet.

About the first of April, Moore called us in from the Plains to go up the river to Ft. Bascom, New Mexico, on a rounding-up expedition. We were gone on that trip over a month.

On our arrival back, Moore went right to work gathering up everything on the range in the shape of cattle, so as to "close-herd" them during the summer. His idea in doing that was to keep them tame. During the winter they had become almost beyond control. The range was too large for so few cattle. And another thing buffalo being so plentiful had a tendency to making them wild.

About the first of June Moore put me in charge of an outfit, which consisted of twenty-five hundred steers, a wagon and cook, four riders, and five horses to the man or rider. He told me to drift over the Plains wherever I felt like, just so I brought the cattle in fat by the time cold weather set in.

It being an unusually wet summer the scores of basins, or "dry lakes," as we called them, contained an abundance of nice fresh water, therefore we would make a fresh camp every few days. The grass was also fine, being mostly buffalo-grass and nearly a foot high. If ever I enjoyed life it was that summer. No flies or mosquitoes to bother, lots of game and a palmy atmosphere.

Towards the latter part of July about ten thousand head of "through" cattle arrived from southern Texas. To keep the "wintered" ones from catching the "Texas fever," Mr. Moore put them all on the Plains, leaving the new arrivals on the north side of the river. There was three herds besides mine. And I was put in charge of the whole outfit, that is, the four herds; although they were held separate as before, with the regular number of men, horses, etc. to each herd.

I then put one of my men in charge of the herd I had been holding, and from that time on until late in the fall I had nothing to do but ride from one herd to the other and see how they were getting along. Some times the camps would be twenty miles apart. I generally counted each bunch once a week, to be certain they were all there.

About the first of October, Moore came out and picked eight hundred of the fattest steers out of the four herds and sent them to Dodge to be shipped to Chicago. He then took everything to the river, to be turned loose onto the winter range until the next spring.

When the hardest work was over—winter camps established, etc., I secured Moore's consent to let me try and overtake the shipping steers and accompany them to Chicago. So mounted on Whisky-peet I struck out, accompanied by one of the boys, John Farris. It was doubtful whether we would overtake the herd before being shipped, as they had already been on the road about fifteen days, long enough to have gotten there.

The night after crossing the Cimeron river we had a little indian scare. About three o'clock that afternoon we noticed two or three hundred mounted reds, off to one side of the road, marching up a ravine in single file. Being only a mile off, John proposed to me that we go over and tackle them for something to eat. We were terribly hungry, as well as thirsty.

I agreed, so we turned and rode towards them. On discovering us they all bunched up, as though parleying. We didn't like such maneuvering, being afraid maybe they were on the war-

106

path, so turned and continued our journey along the road, keeping a close watch behind for fear they might conclude to follow us.

We arrived on Crooked Creek, where there was a store and several ranches, just about dark. On riding up to the store, where we intended stopping all night, we found it vacated, and everything turned up-side down as though the occupants had just left in a terrible hurry. Hearing some ox bells down the creek we turned in that direction, in hopes of finding something to eat.

About a mile's ride brought us to a ranch where several yoke of oxen stood grazing, near the door. Finding a sack of corn in a wagon we fed our horses and then burst open the door of the log house, which was locked. Out jumped a little playful puppy, who had been asleep, his master having locked him up in there, no doubt, in his anxiety to pull for Dodge.

Hanging over the still warm ashes was a pot of nice beef soup which had never been touched. And in the old box cupboard was a lot of cold biscuits and a jar of nice preserves, besides a jug of molasses, etc.

After filling up we struck out for Dodge, still a distance of twenty-five miles. We arrived there a short while after sun-up next morning; and the first man we met—an old friend by the name of Willingham—informed us of the indian outbreak. There had been several men killed on Crooked Creek the evening before—hence John and I finding the ranches deserted.

On riding through the streets that morning, crowds of women, some of them crying, seeing we were just in from the South, flocked around us inquiring for their absent ones, fathers, brothers, lovers and sons, some of whom had already been killed, no doubt; there having been hundreds of men killed in the past few days.

John and I of course laughed in our boots to think that we

turned back, instead of going on to the band of blood-thirsty devils that we had started to go to.

The first thing after putting our horses up at the livery stable, we went to Wright & Beverly's store and deposited our "wealth." John had a draft for one hundred and fourteen dollars, while I had about three hundred and fifty dollars. We then shed our old clothes and crawled into a bran new rig out and out. Erskine Clement, one of Mr. Beal's partners, was in town waiting to ship the herd which should have been there by that time. But he hadn't heard a word from it, since getting Moore's letter—which, by the way, had to go around through Las Vegas, New Mexico, and down through the southern part of Colorado —stating about what time it would arrive in Dodge. He was terribly worried when I informed him that John and I had neither seen nor heard anything of the outfit since it left the ranch.

That night about ten o'clock John, who had struck a lot of his old chums, came and borrowed twenty-five dollars from me, having already spent his one hundred and fourteen dollars that he had when he struck town.

I went to bed early that night, as I had promised to go with Clement early next morning to make a search for the missing herd.

The next morning when Clement and I were fixing to strike out, John came to me, looking bad after his all night rampage, to get his horse and saddle out of "soak." I done so, which cost me thirty-five dollars, and never seen the poor boy afterwards. Shortly after that he went to Ft. Sumner and was killed by one of "Billy the Kid's" men, a fellow by the name of Barney Mason. Thus ended the life of a good man who, like scores of others, let the greatest curse ever known to mankind, whisky, get the upper hand of him.

Clement and I pulled south, our ponies loaded down with

ammunition so in case the indians got us corralled we could stand them off a few days, at least. We were well armed, both having a good winchester and a couple of colts' pistols apiece.

We found the outfit coming down Crooked Creek; they having left the main trail, or road, on the Cimeron, and came over a much longer route, to avoid driving over a dry stretch of country, forty miles between water. Hence John and I missing them. No doubt but that it was a lucky move in them taking that route, for, on the other, they would have just about come in contact with the three or four hundred Cheyenne reds, whose bloody deeds are still remembered in that country.

On arriving in town with the herd we split it in two, making four hundred head in each bunch, and put one half on the cars to be shipped to Chicago. I accompanied the first lot, while Clement remained to come on with the next.

In Burlington, Iowa, I met Mr. Beals. We lay there all day feeding and watering the cattle.

On arriving in Chicago, I went right to the Palmer house, but after paying one dollar for dinner I concluded its price too high for a common clod-hopper like myself. So I moved to the Ervin House, close to the Washington Street tunnel, a two dollar a day house.

That night I turned myself loose taking in the town, or at least a little corner of it. I squandered about fifteen dollars that night on boot-blacks alone. Every one of the little imps I met struck me for a dime, or something to eat. They knew, at a glance, from the cut of my jib, that they had struck a bonanza. They continued to "work" me too, during my whole stay in the city. At one time, while walking with Mr. Beals and another gentleman, a crowd of them who had spied me from across the street, yelled "Yonder goes our Texas Ranger! Lets tackle him for some stuff!"

About the third day I went broke, and from that time on I had to borrow from Mr. Beals. I left there about a hundred dollars in his debt.

After spending six days in the city I left for Dodge City, Kansas, in company with Mr. Beals and Erskine Clement, who, instead of stopping at Dodge, continued on to Grenada, Colorado, where the "Beals Cattle Co." still held their headquarters.

Arriving in Dodge City, I found Whisky-peet, whom I had left in Anderson's stable, all O. K., and mounting him I struck out all alone for the "L. X." ranch, two hundred and twenty-five miles.

Arriving at the ranch I found the noted "Billy the Kid" and his gang there. Among his daring followers were the afterwards noted Tom O'Phalliard, and Henry Brown, leader of the Medicine Lodge Bank tragedy which happened in 1884, who was shot in trying to escape, while his three companions were hung. "The Kid" was there trying to dispose of a herd of ponies he had stolen from the "Seven River warriors" in Lincoln County, New Mexico—his bitter enemies whom he had fought so hard against, that past summer, in what is known as the "bloody Lincoln County war of '78." During his stay at the ranch and around Tascosa, I became intimately acquainted with him and his jovial crowd. I mention these facts because I intend to give you a brief sketch of Billy's doings, in the closing pages of this book.

# 19. A LONELY RIDE OF
# ELEVEN HUNDRED MILES

AFTER laying around the ranch a couple of weeks, Mr. Moore put me in charge of a scouting outfit and sent me out on the South Plains to drift about all winter, watching for cattle thieves, etc.; also to turn back any cattle that might slip by the "sign riders" and drift across the Plains.

During that winter we, that is my crowd, went to church several times. A little Colony of Christians headed by the Rev. Cahart, had settled on the head of Salt Fork, a tributary of Red river, and built a church house in which the little crowd, numbering less than fifty souls would congregate every Sunday and pray.

That same little church house now ornaments the thriving little city of Clarendon, County seat of Donley County. The old inhabitants point to it with pride when telling of how it once stood solitary and alone out on the great buffalo range two hundred miles from nowhere.

The Colony had come from Illinois and drifted away out there beyond the outskirts of civilization to get loose from that demon whisky. And early that coming spring a lot of ruffians started a saloon in their midst. A meeting was called in the little church house and resolutions passed to drive them out, if in no other way, with powder and lead. They pulled their freight and I am proud to state that I had a hand in making them pull it; for the simple reason that they had no business encroaching upon those good people's rights.

When spring opened Mr. Moore called me in from the Plains and put me in charge of a rounding-up outfit, which consisted of twelve riders and a cook.

To begin rounding-up, we went over to Canyon Paladuro, where Chas. Goodnight had a ranch, and where a great many of the river cattle had drifted during the winter. There was about a hundred men and seven or eight wagons in the outfit that went over. We stopped over Sunday in the little Christian Colony and went to church. The Rev. Cahart preached about the wild and woolly Cow Boy of the west; how the eastern people had him pictured off as a kind of animal with horns, etc. While to him, looking down from his dry goods box pulpit into the manly faces of nearly a hundred of them, they looked just like human beings, minus the standing collar, etc.

About the first of July, Moore sent me to Nickerson, Kansas, with a herd of eight hundred shipping steers. My outfit consisted of five men, a chuck wagon, etc. Our route lay over a wild strip of country where there was no trails nor scarcely any ranches—that is, until reaching the southern line of Kansas.

We arrived at Nickerson after being on the road two months. "Deacon" Bates, Mr. Beals partner, was there waiting for us. He had come through with several herds that had left the ranch a month ahead of us. He was still holding some of the poorest ones, south of town, where he had a camp established.

After loading my wagon with a fresh supply of grub, Mr. Bates, or the "Deacon" as he was more commonly called, sent me back over the trail he and his outfits had come, to gather lost steers—some they had lost coming through.

I was gone about a month and came back with eighteen head. We had a soft trip of it, as most of our hard work was such as buying butter, eggs, etc., from the scattering grangers along the Kansas border. We never missed a meal on the trip, and always had the best the country afforded, regardless of cost. Deacon Bates was always bragging on some of his bosses, how cheap they could live, etc. I just thought I would try him this time, being in a country where luxuries were plentiful, and see if he wouldn't blow on me as being a person with good horse sense. An animal of course, as we all know, will eat the choicest grub he can get; and why not man, when he is credited with having more sense than the horse, one of the most intellectual animals that exists?

On our return to Nickerson, I concluded to quit and spend the winter with mother, whom I received letters from every now and then begging me to come home. As I wasn't certain of coming back, I thought it best to go overland and take Whisky-peet along, for I couldn't even bear the *thought* of parting with him; and to hire a car to take him around by rail would be too costly.

I got all ready to start and then went to Deacon Bates for a settlement. He took my account book and, after looking it over, said: "Why, Dum it to h——l, I can't pay no such bills as those! Why, Dum-it all, old Jay Gould would groan under the weight of these bills!" He then went on to read some of the items aloud. They ran as follows: Cod-fish $10; eggs $40; butter $70; milk $5; bacon $150; flour $200; canned fruits $400; sundries $600, etc., etc. Suffice it to say, the old gent told me in plain Yankee English that I would have to go in Chicago and settle with Mr. Beals. I hated the idea of going to Chicago, for I knew my failings—I was afraid I wouldn't have money enough left when I got back to pay my expenses home.

That same evening a letter came from Mr. Beals stating that he had just received a letter from Moore, at the ranch, in which he informed him that there were two more herds on the trail for Nickerson, and, as it was getting so near winter, for Joe Hargraves, better known as "Jinglebob Joe," and I to go and turn them to Dodge City, the nearest shipping point.

After putting Whisky-peet and my "Missouri" mare, one I had bought to use as a pack-horse going home, in care of an old granger to be fed and taken good care of until my return, Joe and I struck out with only one horse apiece—just the ones we were riding.

On our arrival in Dodge I pulled out for Chicago, to get a settlement, with the first train load we shipped. I took my saddle, bridle, spurs, etc. along and left them in Atchison, Mo., the first point we stopped to feed at, until my return.

Arriving in Chicago, I told Mr. Beals that I was going home to spend the winter, and therefore wanted to settle up.

He set 'em up to a fine Havana and then proceeded. Every time he came to one of those big bills, which caused the Deacon's eyes to bulge out, he would grunt and crack about a forty-cent smile, but never kicked.

When he had finished there was a few hundred dollars to my credit. He then asked me if I could think of anything else that I had forgotten to charge the "company" with? Of course I couldn't, because I didn't have time; his question was put to me too sudden. If I could have had a few hours to myself, to figure the thing up just right, I think I could have satisfied the old Gent.

I remained in the city three days taking in the sights and feeding the hungry little boot blacks. When leaving, Mr. Beals informed me that he was going to buy a lot of southern Texas cattle, to put on his Panhandle ranch, the coming spring, and if I wanted a job, to hold myself in readiness to boss one of the herds up the trail for him. Of course that just suited me, providing I couldn't make up my mind to remain at home.

114

Landing in Nickerson I hired a horse and went out to the old granger's ranch where I had left my two ponies. They were both fat and feeling good.

Before starting out on my little journey of only eleven hundred miles, I bought a pack-saddle and cooking outfit—that is, just a frying pan, small coffee pot, etc. I used the mare for a pack animal and rode Whisky-peet. I had just six dollars left when I rode out of Nickerson.

I went through Fort Reno and Fort Sill, Indian territory and crossed Red river into Texas on the old military road, opposite Henrietta.

When within ten miles of Denton, Texas, on Pecan creek, Whisky-peet became lame—so much so that he could scarcely walk. I was stopping over night with a Mr. Cobb, and next morning I first noticed his lameness.

I lacked about twenty-five cents of having enough to pay Mr. Cobb for my night's lodging that morning. I had sold my watch for five dollars a short while before and now that was spent.

Whisky-peet being too lame to travel, I left him with Mr. Cobb while I rode into Denton to try and make a raise of some money.

I tried to swap my mare off for a smaller animal and get some boot, but every one seemed to think that she had been stolen; I being so anxious to swap.

I rode back to Mr. Cobb's that night in the same fix, financially, as when I left that morning.

The next day I made a raise of some money. Mr. Cobb and I made a saddle swap, he giving me twenty dollars to boot. He and I also swapped bridles, I getting four dollars and a half to boot. One of his little boys then gave me his saddle and one dollar and a half for my pack-saddle, which had cost me ten dollars in Nickerson. I then had lots of money.

Whisky-peet soon got over his lameness, having just stuck

115

a little snag into the frog of his foot, which I succeeded in finding and pulling out before it had time to do serious damage, and I started on my journey again.

On arriving in Denton that time, a negro struck me for a horse swap right away. I got a three year old pony and six dollars in money for my mare; the pony suited just as well for a pack animal as the mare.

The next day after leaving Denton, I stopped in a negro settlement and won a fifty-dollar horse, running Whisky-peet against a sleepy looking grey. I had up twenty dollars in money and my Winchester, a fine silver mounted gun. I won the race by at least ten open feet, but the negroes tried to swindle me out of it.

While riding along that evening three negroes rode up and claimed the horse I had won. They claimed that the parties who bet him off had no right to him, as they just had borrowed him from one of them to ride to the Settlement that morning. I finally let them have him for twenty dollars.

I went through the following towns after leaving Denton: Ft. Worth, Clenborn, Hillsborough, Waco, Herrene, Bryant, Brenham and Columbus; besides scores of smaller places.

I rode up to mother's little shanty on Cashe's creek after being on the road just a month and twelve days.

To say that mother was glad to see me would only half express it. She bounced me the first thing about not coming back the next fall after leaving as I had promised. I had been gone nearly four years.

## 20. ANOTHER START UP THE CHISHOLM TRAIL

I HADN'T been at home but a few days when I came very near getting killed by a falling house.

Mother had become tired of the neighborhood she lived in and wanted me to move her and her shanty down the creek about a mile, to Mr. Cornelius's. So hiring a yoke of oxen—although a pair of goats would have answered the purpose—I hauled her household goods down to the spot selected. I then went to work tearing the shanty down.

In building it I had set eight pine posts two feet in the ground, and then nailed the sidings, etc., to them. There was only one room and it was eight feet wide and fourteen long. The roof had been made of heavy pine boards. After tearing both ends out, I climbed onto the roof to undo that.

I was a-straddle of the sharp roof, about midway, axe in one hand and a large chisel in the other, when all at once the sides began spreading out at the top. Of course I began sinking slowly but surely, until everything went down with a crash.

The pine posts had become rotten from the top of the ground down; and just as soon as the roof and I had struck bottom the sides flopped over onto us.

A neighbor's little boy by the name of Benny Williams, had been monkeying around watching me work, and unluckily he was inside of the shanty when the collapse came.

I was sensible, but unable to move, there being so much weight on me.

Finally little Benny who was one thickness of boards under me woke up and began squalling like a six months old calf being put through the process of branding.

After squalling himself hoarse he began to moan most pitiously. That was too much for me. I could stand his bleating but his moaning for help put new life into my lazy muscles, causing me to exert every nerve in my body, so as to get out and render the poor boy assistance. I had, before the boy's cries disturbed me, made up my mind to lie still and wait for something to turn up.

In exerting myself I found that I could move my body down towards my feet, an inch at a time. The weight was all on my left shoulder. But it soon came in contact with something else, which relieved my bruised shoulder of most of the weight.

I got out finally after a long and painful struggle; and securing help from the Morris ranch, fished Benny out. He had one leg broken below the knee, besides other bruises. I was slightly disfigured, but still in the ring.

I put in the winter visiting friends, hunting, etc. I had sold my cattle—the mavricks branded nearly four years before—to Mr. Geo. Hamilton, at the market price, from five to ten dollars a head, according to quality, to be paid for when he got his own brand put on to them. Every now and then he would brand a few, and with the money received for them I would buy grub and keep up my dignity.

About the first of March I received a letter from Mr. Rosencrans, one of D. T. Beals' partners, stating that Mr. Beals had bought his cattle in middle Texas instead of southern as he had expected, and as he had told me in Chicago. "But," continued the letter, "we have bought a herd from Charles Word of Goliad, on the San Antonia River, to be delivered at our Panhandle ranch and have secured you the job of bossing it. Now should you wish to come back and work for us, go out and report to Mr. Word at once."

The next day I kissed mother good-bye, gave Whisky peet a hug, patted Chief—a large white dog that I had picked up in the Indian Territory on my way through—a few farewell pats on the head, mounted "Gotch"—a pony I had swapped my star-spangled winchester for—and struck out for Goliad, ninety miles west. Leaving Whisky-peet behind was almost as severe on me as having sixteen jawteeth pulled. I left him, in Horace Yeamans' care, so that I could come back by rail the coming fall. I failed to come back though that fall as I expected, therefore never got to see the faithful animal again; he died the following spring.

A three days' ride brought me to Goliad, the place where Fannin and his brave followers met their sad fate during the Mexican war. It was dark when I arrived there. After putting up my horse, I learned from the old gent Mr. Word, who was a saddler, and whom I found at work in his shop, that his son Charlie was out at Beeville, gathering a bunch of cattle.

Next morning I struck out for Beeville, thirty miles west, arriving there about four o'clock in the afternoon.

About sun-down I found Charles Word, and his crowd of muddy cow-punchers, five miles west of town. They were almost up to their ears in mud, (it having been raining all day,) trying to finish "road-branding" that lot of steers before dark. The corral having no "chute" the boys had to rope and wrestle with the wild brutes until the hot iron could be applied to their wet and muddy sides.

When I rode up to the corral, Charlie came out, and I introduced myself. He shook my hand with a look of astonishment on his brow, as much to say, I'll be——if Beals mustn't be crazy, sending this smooth-faced kid here to take charge of a herd for me! He finally after talking awhile told me that I would have to work under Mr. Stephens, until we got ready to put up the Beals herd—or at least the one I was to accompany. He also told me to keep the boys from knowing that I was going to boss the next herd, as several of them were fishing for the job, and might become stubborn should they know the truth.

I went on "night-guard" after supper and it continued to rain all night, so that I failed to get any sleep; but then I didn't mind it, as I was well rested.

The next day after going to work, was when I caught fits though, working in a muddy pen all day. When night came I didn't feel as much like going on guard as I did the night before. A laughable circumstance happened that morning after going into the branding-pen.

As the pen had no "chute" we had to rope and tie down, while applying the brand. The men working in pairs, one, which ever happened to get a good chance, to catch the animal by both fore feet as he run by which would "bump" him, that is, capsize him. The other fellow would then be ready to jump aboard and hold him until securely fastened. There being only seven of us to do the roping that morning, it of course left one man without a "pard," and that one was me. Each one you see is always anxious to get a good roper for a "pard," as then everything works smoothly. Mr. Word told me to sit on the fence and rest until Ike Word, an old negro who used to belong to the Word family, and who was the best roper in the crowd, returned from town where he had been sent with a message.

It wasn't long till old Ike galloped up, wearing a broad grin. He was very anxious to get in the pen and show "dem fellers de art of cotching um by boaf front feet." But when his boss told him he would have to take me for a "pard" his broad grin vanished. Calling Mr. Word to one side he told him that he didn't want that yankee for a "pard," as he would have to do all the work, etc. He was told to try me one round and if I didn't suit he could take some one else. Shortly afterwards while passing Mr. Word old Ike whispered and said: "Dogon me if dat yankee don't surprise de natives!" When night came, and while I was on herd, old Ike sat around the camp fire wondering to the other boys "whar dat yankee learned to rope so well." You see Mr. Word had told the boys that I was from the Panhandle, and old Ike thought the Panhandle was way up in Yankeedom somewhere, hence he thinking I was a yankee. A few days after that though, I satisfied old Ike that I was a thoroughbred.

Mr. Word bought a bunch of ponies, new arrivals from Mexico, and among them was a large iron-grey, which the mexicans had pointed out as being "Muncho Deablo." None of the boys, not even old Ike, cared to tackle him. So one morning I caught and saddled him. He fought like a tiger while being saddled; and after getting it securely fastened he threw it off and stamped it into a hundred pieces, with his front feet, which caused me to have to buy a new one next day. I then borrowed Mr. Stephens' saddle, and after getting securely seated in it, raised the blinds and gave him the full benefit of spurs and quirt. After pitching about half a mile, me, saddle and all went up in the air, the girths having broken. But having the "hackimore" rope fastened to my belt I held to him until help arrived. I then borrowed another saddle, and this time stayed with him. From that on, old Ike recognized me as a genuine cow-puncher.

We finally got that herd, of thirty-seven hundred steers, ready for the trail; but the very night after getting them counted and ready to turn over to Mr. Stephens the next morning, they stampeded, half of them getting away and mixing up with thousands of other cattle.

Mr. Stephens thought he would try a new scheme that trip up the trail, so he bought a lot of new bulls-eye lanterns to be used around the herd on dark, stormy nights, so that each man could tell just where the other was stationed by the reflection of his light.

This night in question being very dark and stormy, Stephens thought he would christen his new lamps. He gave me one, although I protested against such nonsense.

About ten o'clock some one suddenly flashed his bulls-eye towards the herd, and off they went, as though shot out of a gun.

In running my horse at full speed in trying to get to the lead, or in front of them, me, horse, bulls-eye and all went over an old rail fence—where there had once been a ranch—in a pile. I put the entire blame onto the lamp, the light of which had blinded my horse so that he didn't see the fence.

I wasn't long in picking myself up and mounting my horse who was standing close by, still trembling from the shock he received. I left the lamp where it lay, swearing vengeance against the use of them, around cattle, and dashed off after the flying herd.

When daylight came I and a fellow by the name of Glass, found ourselves with about half of the herd, at least ten miles from camp. The rest of the herd was scattered all over the country, badly mixed up with other cattle. It took us several days to get the lost ones gathered, and the herd in shape again.

After bidding Stephens and the boys who were to accompany

him, adieu, to meet again on Red River where he was to wait for us, we pulled for Goliad to rig up a new outfit, horses, wagon, etc.

The horses, Word bought out of a mexican herd which had just arrived from Old Mexico. He gave eighteen dollars a head for the choice, out of several hundred head.

Being all ready to start for Kimble County, two hundred miles northwest, where the herd was to be gathered, Mr. Word turned the outfit over to me, while he went around by stage.

## 21. A TRIP WHICH TERMINATED IN THE CAPTURE OF "BILLY THE KID"

WE WENT through San Antonio and lay there long enough to have all of our horses shod, as we were going into a mountainous country where they couldn't stand it without shoes. While there I visited the Almo building where poor Davy Crocket and his brave companions bit the dust.

We arrived at our destination, Joe Taylor's ranch, on Paint creek a small tributary to the Llano, at last; and it was one of the roughest, rockiest, God-forsaken countries I ever put foot on.

We finally, after three weeks hard work, got the herd of twenty-five hundred head started towards the north star. We were awful glad to get out of there too, for our horses were all nearly peetered out, and the men on the war-path, from having to work twenty-six hours a day.

At Red river we overtook Stephens and changed herds with him, his being the ones to go to Beal's ranch, while the others were for the Wyoming market.

After parting with Stephens again we turned in a northwesterly direction and arrived at the "L. X." ranch on the first day of July.

Moore sent me right out on the Plains to hold the herd I came up with, until fall. That just suited me as I needed a rest.

After turning the herd loose on the range about the first of September, I was put in charge of a branding outfit. Our work then was drifting over the range branding calves.

Late in the fall when all the branding was done, Moore put me in charge of a scouting outfit and sent me out on the Plains to drift around, the same as previous winters.

I hadn't been there long, though, when he sent word for me to turn my outfit over to James McClaughety and come in to the ranch; and to bring three of my picked men along.

On arriving at the ranch I found that he wanted me to take an outfit and go to New Mexico after a lot of cattle that "Billy the Kid" had stolen and run over there.

The cattlemen along the Canadian river had hired a fellow by the name of Frank Stuart to keep a lookout for stolen cattle in New Mexico; and along in the summer he came to the Panhandle and notified the different cattlemen who had him employed that "Billy the Kid" and his gang were making a regular business of stealing Panhandle cattle and selling them to an old fellow named Pat Cohglin who had a large ranch on Three rivers, close to Ft. Stanton.

The outfits then made up a crowd between them, and sent with Stuart, giving him orders to go right to the Cohglin ranch and take all the cattle found there, in their brands.

But Mr. Stuart failed to go nearer than forty miles from where the cattle were reported to be. He claimed that Cohglin, who had a blood-thirsty crowd around him, sent him word that if he got the cattle he would have to take some hot lead with them, or something to that effect. So Stuart came back, claiming he didn't have men enough.

This made Moore mad, so he concluded to rig up an outfit of his own and send them over after the cattle, hence he sending out after me.

My outfit, after getting it rigged up, consisted of a chuck wagon with four good mules to pull it, a cook and five picked men, named as follows: James East, Lee Hall, Lon Chambers, Cal Pope and last but not by any means least "Big-foot Wallace." They all, except me, had one extra good horse apiece; I had two. Moore thought it best not to have many horses to feed, as corn would be scarce and high. He thought it best to buy more if we needed them.

On starting, Moore gave me these orders: "Stay over there until you get those cattle or bust the "L. X." company. I will keep you supplied in money just as long as they have got a nickel left, that I can get hold of. And when you get the cattle if you think you can succeed in capturing "Billy the Kid" do so. You can hire all the men you need; but don't undertake his capture until you have first secured the cattle."

At Tascosa we met Stuart who had succeeded in raising a little crowd to join us. Mr. McCarty, boss of the "L. I. T." ranch had furnished five men, a cook and chuck wagon; and Torry, whose ranch was further up the river, a wagon and two men, while a man by the name of Johnson furnished a man and wagon. The "L. I T." outfit was in charge of a fellow by the name of "Bob" Roberson, whose orders were to get the stolen cattle before trying to capture the Kid, but in the meantime, to be governed by Stuart's orders. This placed "Bob" in bad shape, as you will see later.

Stuart, after we all got strung out, took the "buck-board" on the mail line, and went on ahead to Las Vegas to put in a week or so with his solid girl.

On arriving at San Lorenzo, New Mexico, I mounted a buck-board and struck out ahead, to Las Vegas, to buy a lot of corn, grub, ammunition, etc., to be delivered at Anton Chico, twenty-five miles south of "Vegas," by the time the crowd got there, so as not to cause any delay. "Bob" Roberson also gave me money to buy a lot of stuff for his outfit.

Arriving in Vegas, during a severe snow storm, I found there wasn't fifty bushels of corn in town, the snow storm having delayed the freight trains. One merchant had just got a bill of several car loads which he expected to arrive any minute. So I concluded I would wait—and help Stuart hold the town down.

I wrote a letter to Anton Chico, telling the boys to lay there and take it easy, as I might be detained several days waiting for corn.

Every morning I would go to the grain merchant, and receive this reply: "Am looking for it every minute; t'will certainly be here by night."

Not being acquainted in town, time passed off very slowly, so I finally got to "bucking" at my old favorite game—monte. I won for a while, but finally my luck took a turn and I lost nearly every dollar I had in my possession, most of which belonged to my employers. The one hundred dollars that "Bob" Roberson gave to buy stuff for his outfit, also went.

While standing over the exciting game, after my pile had dwindled down to an even seventy dollars, I put just half of it, thirty-five dollars, on the Queen, or "horse," as it is called, being the picture of a woman on horseback, and made a vow, if I lost that bet that I never would as long as I lived, "buck" at monte again. I lost, and my vow has been sacredly kept.

The corn finally arrived, but having no money, I had to run my face by giving an order on the "L. X." company, payable on demand. The other stuff, ammunition, etc., also things "Bob" had sent for, I had to buy in the same manner. Of course I hated to give orders so soon after leaving the ranch with a pocketfull of money, but then that was the best I could do under existing circumstances.

After getting the goods started for Anton Chico, Stuart and I hired a rig and followed.

Arriving in "Chico" we found Barney Mason, (an ex-chum

of the "Kid's," but now a deputy sheriff under Pat Garrett) there, with a message from Garrett telling Stuart to meet him in Vegas at a certain date, on important business. So Stuart struck right back to Vegas, accompanied by Mason, as the date fixed was only a few days off.

I found the boys all well and having a fat time. The only thing that bothered me they had run in debt head over heels on the strength of me having lots of money. The merchants expected their pay according to contract, immediately after my arrival. I had to satisfy them with orders on the "L. X." firm.

The boys had lots of news to relate, things that had happened after I left: One of "Bob's" men had had a shooting scrape with some mexicans; and "Billy the Kid" and his crowd has been in town, they having come in afoot, and went out well mounted. He and his five men having hoofed it through deep snow from the Greathouse ranch, over a hundred miles southwest of there.

After getting everything in shape we pulled out for White Oaks, one hundred and fifty miles southwest.

The second night out we camped at the Lewelling Wells, where bright and early next morning Stuart overtook us; accompanied by Pat Garrett and Barney Mason. They came with a scheme all cut and dried, by which they could get the big reward offered for the "Kid." Garrett knew the Kid and his few remaining followers had been to Chico and left for Fort Sumner a few days before; and that they were wore out from having been chased all over the country by a gang of ninety men from White Oaks and vicinity. Now was his time to strike, if he could just get Stuart to go in cahoots with him. That was soon accomplished; a promise of half of the reward, I suppose, done the work. Hence he sending for Stuart to come and see him in "Vegas" on important business.

After eating breakfast Stuart broke the ice by telling a lie. He knew our orders were strictly to get the cattle first, and then

128

if we could assist in the capture of the "Kid" to do so. Therefore he branched out thus: "Well boys, we have got a job on our hands: 'Kid' is on his way to Old Mexico with a bunch of Panhandle cattle; and we want every man in the outfit, except just enough to accompany the wagons to White Oaks, to go with Garrett and I to overtake them."

"How can that be," someone asked "when Kid and his men just left Anton Chico a few days ago?"

"Don't know," was the quick answer, unless some of his outfit had the cattle under herd somewhere down the river waiting for him. If you doubt my word about it, just ask Mr. Garrett, there.

Of course we all did doubt his word, and were well satisfied that it was a put up job, to gain the reward.

"Bob" Roberson and I went to one side and talked the matter over, while Stuart and his little party remained at camp wondering whether their little scheme would have strength to hold out, on its weak legs or not.

"Bob" was in favor, after we had talked the thing over, of going right back and telling Stuart in plain English that he lied. But I wouldn't agree to that for fear it might accidently be true. I thought it strange that Garrett, who had the reputation of being a model of a man, would sit by with his mouth shut and listen to such a falsehood. Of course Garrett couldn't be blamed very much for he, being Sheriff, was interested in the "Kid's" capture, no matter what became of the cattle we had come after.

"Bob" and I finally concluded, for fear the statement might be true, to let them have a few men, but not enough to completely cripple us so that we couldn't go on after the cattle should we think it best, after getting to White Oaks.

I let them take three out of my crowd: "Jim East, "Lon" Chambers and "Lee" Hall. While "Bob" gave up two, "Tom"

Emory and Louis Bozman. Stuart wasn't satisfied, he wanted more. But not being successful in getting his whole wants supplied, they all rode off down the Pecos valley.

Shortly after they left we pulled out on the White Oaks road. That night it began to snow, and kept it up for several days until the whole ground was covered to the depth of from two to three feet; so that it was slow work getting our wagons along through it.

A few days afterwards we came to the Greathouse ranch, or at least to the hot ashes where it once stood, where "Kid" and six of his daring followers were surrounded by ninety men one whole night and day. It was as follows:

A squad of men left White Oaks to hunt the "Kid" who was lurking in the neighborhood. They suddenly came upon him and Bill Willson cooking their breakfasts, one morning.

On discovering their enemies they both, after firing a shot apiece, sped through the mountains like deer, leaving their horses, saddles, coats and breakfast behind.

One of the shots fired at the White Oaks party took effect in the brain of a good horse that a young man by the name of Johnny Hudgens was riding, while the other, went through a hat, on the head of a young man.

After following the trail through the deep snow awhile, and after satisfying themselves that the two young outlaws couldn't hide their tracks, the party struck back to White Oaks after something to eat, and more men.

When they returned, that same evening, there was ninety men in the crowd. They got on the trail and followed it, until shortly after dark, when it brought them to within a few hundred yards of the Greathouse ranch, on the "Vegas" and White Oaks road.

To satisfy themselves that the game was bagged, they circled around the ranch to see that no trails were leading out from it.

They then stationed themselves in a circle around the house and, dismounting, began to make breast-works out of pine logs— the ranch being in the midst of a large pine grove.

When day-light came Greathouse sent a negro who was stopping with him, out after the horses which had been hobbled the night before.

Mr. "Nig" hadn't gone but a few hundred yards when he was captured by the White Oaks boys.

After learning from him that the "Kid" and five of his men were in the house they sent him back with a note to the "Kid," telling him if he and his party would come out with their hands up they would be treated as prisoners of war; if not they would have to stand the consequences, etc.

In a few minutes the negro returned with a note from the "Kid," stating: "You fellers go to h——ll!" or something to that effect.

A consultation was then held, and finally decided to give the boys one more chance for their lives, before storming the house. So they sent Mr. Coon back with another note stating, that that would be their last chance, etc.

In a short while a new messenger came forward. It was "Jim" Greathouse, proprietor of the ranch. He stated that the "Kid" desired to have a talk with their leader. On asking him what assurance he could give that their leader wouldn't be harmed, he replied, "myself." He told them that they could hold him a prisoner, and if anything happened to Carlyle, he was willing to stand the consequences.

So Mr. "Jim" Carlyle, he being the leader, marched forward —never more to return—to have a talk with the "Kid."

Arriving in the house where there was also a saloon, kept there to accommodate the thirsty traveler, he was made to go up to the bar and drink "health to Billy the Kid." This of course went against the grain with "Jim," but then what else could he do now, being at their mercy?                                    131

Finally the Kid spied one of the gloves he had left behind in his retreat the day before, sticking out of "Jim's" coat pocket.

This revived the hardships he and Billy Willson were compelled to endure, nearly all day the day before, traveling through snow up to their knees. So pulling the glove out of "Jim's" pocket and holding it up at arms length, he asked: "Jim, was you with that mob yesterday who caused me such a tramp through the snow?"

"Yes," was the answer.

"Well then, come up and take your last drink on this earth, for I am going to blow your light out."

"Jim" of course didn't relish the half pint of rot-gut that he was forced to drink at the point of a colts "45."

After drinking a full glass himself the "Kid" threw his pistol down in "Jim's" face, full cocked, telling him at the same time to say his prayers while he slowly counted "three."

The "one, two, three!" was uttered, and then a pistol shot rang out upon the still air, re-echoing from the mountain sides, in every direction.

The bullet had struck its mark, a tin can hanging on the wall a few inches above "Jim's" head.

"Well, Jim," was the first words that broke the death-like silence within, "you are worth several dead men yet, ain't you?" Said "Kid" grabbing "Jim's" trembling hand and leading him up to the bar, over which Billy Willson handed the fiery bug-juice.

"You didn't think I would be brute enough to shoot you in *such* a cowardly manner, did you, Jim?" continued the "Kid" setting his empty glass down on the counter.

The shot from within had excited the crowd out side almost to fever heat; they thinking that it meant their leaders' death. One fellow during the exciting moment scribbled off a note which read thus: "If Carlyle ain't out here in ten minutes by the watch, your friend Greathouse will be a corpse," and sent it to the "Kid" by the negro, who had returned after delivering the last message which brought Greathouse out.

The note was read in the presence of Carlyle, so that he heard every word it contained.

"Kid" then answered it by stating: "Carlyle is safe, but we can't give him up just yet. Now remember, if we hear a shot from the outside we will take it for granted that you have carried out your threats by killing Greathouse, and will have to pay you back by killing our prisoner," etc.

"Jim" knew the substance of the note and trembled in his boots at the thoughts of an accident shot being fired by his party. He was satisfied that his men wouldn't do as they threatened in the note after hearing, from the negro's own lips, that he was still alive. It was the *accident* shot that disturbed his mind.

The negro hadn't more than got behind the breast-works with the note when a man, stationed behind another breastwork, who knew nothing of the threat having been made, fired a shot at the house "just for fun."

Carlyle, on hearing the shot, made a leap at the only glass window in the house, taking sash and all with him. But before striking the ground several bullets from the "Kids" well aimed "45" had pierced his body. He crawled a few yards and then fell over dead, in plain view of his eighty odd companions.

"Kid" claimed afterwards that he was sorry for having had to kill "Jim." Their intentions were to hold him prisoner until dark, when they would tie him down, so he couldn't give the alarm, and then make their escape.

From that on, the mad crowd outside kept up a continued firing at the log house until dark. But doing no damage, as the boys had breast-works built of sacks of flour, boxes, bedding, etc.

Jim Greathouse during the excitement gave his guards the

slip and pulled for "tall timber" up in the mountains where it was almost impossible for a mounted man to follow. I have often afterwards heard Greathouse laugh over the matter and tell how he "just hit the high places," and beat Goldsmith Maid's fastest time, for the first half mile.

About ten o'clock that night the White Oaker's began to get tired and hungry, so concluded they would go back to town, forty miles, fill up, get a fresh mount and return by daylight, without the "Kid" and his men knowing anything of it. They stole off very slyly, without making any noise, and when they got about a mile, put their horses down to their best licks.

About midnight the little party inside made a bold break for liberty. They headed north-east, with cocked winchesters, determined on fighting their way out. But they were happily disappointed.

A ten-mile tramp through snow brought them to the Spencer ranch, which was kept by a kind old man by the name of Spencer, who lived there all alone, and was trying to establish a shorter route from "Vegas" to the "Oaks" by turning the road by his place, where there was a fine spring of water, a luxury the Greathouse ranch lacked, they having to haul water a distance of several miles from up in the rough mountains.

Just as day was breaking the crowd returned from the "Oaks," and finding their game had fled they set fire to the house and struck out on the newly made foot prints.

Arriving at the Spencer ranch they learned, from the old gentleman, that the "Kid" and his little party of five had been gone about two hours, and that they had eaten breakfast with him.

After continuing on the trail about an hour longer, until it brought them to a rough strip of country where they would be compelled to take it afoot, they gave up the chase, and turned back to take their spite out on poor old Spencer for feeding the "Kid" and his crowd.

They took the poor old harmless fellow out to a neighboring tree, after setting fire to his ranch, and put a rope around his neck; but before they had time to swing him up, a few of the men, who had been opposed from the start, interfered in the old man's behalf. Thus his neck was saved, and he is to-day a highly respected citizen in that community, which has since that time become a rich mining district.

The "Kid" and his men made it into Anton Chico, where, as I stated before, they stole a good horse and saddle apiece, while the boys were there waiting for me to arrive from "Vegas," and pulled down the Reo Pecos.

## 22. BILLY THE KID'S CAPTURE

W E ARRIVED in the beautifully located town of White Oaks on the 23d day of December, (1880). The town, which consisted of 1000 inhabitants, mostly American miners, was then not quite two years old and pretty lively for its age. It contained eight saloons; and Saturday nights when the boys would come in from the surrounding mountains, to spend the Sabbath, is when the little burg would put on city airs.

We rented a large log house in the lower end of town and went to living like white folks. We had no money, but we struck two of the merchants who gave us an unlimited credit until we could make a raise. Our greatest expense was feeding the horses corn which cost five cents a pound and hay, two cents a pound. The grub we ate wasn't very expensive as we stole all of our meat, and shared with our honest neighbors who thought it a great sin to kill other people's cattle. You see "Bob" and I still clung to the old Texas style which is, never kill one of your own beeves when you can get somebody else's.

We had concluded not to go after the stolen cattle until the rest of the boys got there, by which time the deep snow would be melted, maybe, so that we could scour the White Mountains, where the cattle were reported to be, out thoroughly.

New-Year's night we had a bushel of fun making the citizens think that "Billy the Kid" had taken the town. Billy was in the habit of "shooting the town up a lot" every now and then, hence, every time a few dozen shots were fired at an unusually late hour, they putting it down as being some of his devilment.

We first sent one of our crowd up-town to the billiard hall, where most of the men generally congregated, and especially "Pinto Tom," the marshal, whose maneuvers we were anxious to learn, to watch and see what kind of an effect our shooting had on the people.

At precisely twelve o'clock we got out with winchesters and six-shooters, cooks and all, and turned ourselves loose. About one hundred shots were fired in quick succession. We then went up town to note the effect.

Arriving at the billiard hall we found old "Uncle Jimmie," our man, standing in the door laughing fit to kill himself. The hall was empty, with the exception of a few who were still hid under tables, chairs, etc. Most of them had gone out of the back door, there being a rough canyon within a few yards of it leading to the mountains, right at the marshal's heels. It was said that "Pinto Tom" didn't get in from the mountains for two days, and when he did come, he swore he had been off prospecting.

Shortly after New-Years some of our men arrived, bringing the news of the "Kid's" capture, while the rest, Jim East and Tom Emory had accompanied Garrett and Stuart to "Vegas" with the prisoners.

Stuart sent a letter by one of the boys, stating that he, East and Emory, would be in the "Oaks" just as quick as they could get there, after turning the prisoners over to the authorities in "Vegas."

So, knowing that we were destined to remain around the "Oaks" a week or two at least, we pulled out in the mountains and camped, so as to save expenses by letting our horses eat grass instead of hay.

That night, after the boys arrived and after we had moved camp out in the timber, while seated around a blazing pinyon fire, Lon Chambers who was a splendid single-handed talker, began relating how they captured the "Kid," etc., which ran about this way, as near as I can remember:

"After leaving you fellers we caught——. It began snowing that night, and kept it up for two or three days and nights.

Arriving in Ft. Sumner, Garrett got word that the Kid and outfit would be in town that night from Los Potales, where the 'Kid's' ranch or cave was situated, so he secured a house near the road leading to 'Potales,' to secret his men in. He then kept a man out doors, on guard, watching the road.

"About ten o'clock that night, while we were all inside playing a five-cent game of poker, the guard opened the door and said, 'Garrett, here comes a crowd down the road!' We all dashed out, winchesters in hand, and hid behind an adobe fence, close by, which they would be compelled to pass.

The moon was shining and we could tell who it was, or at least Garrett and Mason could; they being well acquainted with them. There was six in the approaching crowd, and thirteen of us.

When they rode up within speaking distance Garrett yelled, 'throw up your hands!' His voice had hardly died out when thirteen shots from our nervously gripped winchesters were fired into their midst.

When the smoke cleared off we found that they had all vanished, with the exception of Tom Ophalliard who was mortally wounded, and died shortly after. He had several bullet holes through his body. 'These,' pointing down to his feet, 'are his

over shoes, and this' pulling off a finely finished mexican sombraro and displaying it, "is the hat I pulled from his head before he had quit kicking."

"The next morning we struck out on the trail which led back
towards Los Potales. The white snow along the trail was red
with blood, having flowed from the wounds in Rudabaugh's
horse. The poor animal died though after carrying his heavy
master through twelve miles of deep snow.

About midnight we hove in sight of a little rock house standing on the banks of a small arroyo. The trail led right up to the
door which faced the south. Right near the door stood four shivering horses.

Knowing we had the little band trapped, we took things cool
until daylight, when we stationed ourselves around the house.

There being no opening in the building except the door, Garrett and Lee Hall crawled up to the end wall so they could
watch the door from around the corner, while the rest of us con-
cealed ourselves behind knolls, etc.

We had left our horses behind a hill quite a distance from
the house.

When it became light enough to see, Charlie Bowdre stepped
out doors to see about his horse, but he hadn't more than hit
the ground when two bullets, fired by Garrett and Hall, who
were still at the corner not a dozen feet from the door, sent him
to his long home. He only uttered a few words, which were: 'I
wish, I wish,' before his last breath left him.

Of course that caused a stirring around inside; they knew
what it meant and began making preparations for an escape.
The 'Kid' had his pony inside, out of the cold and the other
four—Rudabaugh having secured another one—were tied to the
door frame so that they could reach the ropes without exposing
their bodies. Now thought they if we can pull three of the horses
inside we will mount and make a bold dash out of the door. But

when they got the first animal about half way into the house Garrett sent a bullet through its heart. The dead animal of course blocked the way so that they had to give up that scheme.

They then tried picking port holes through the thick rock walls, but had to give it up also, as they had nothing to do it with but their knives and fire-arms.

The 'Kid' and Garrett finally opened up a conversation. The former seemed to be in fine humor. Every now and then he would crack some kind of a joke and then laugh, so that every one of us could hear him. At one time he asked in a jovial way: 'Garrett, have you got a fire out there?' 'Yes, a good one!' was the answer. 'Can we come out and warm if we behave ourselves?' 'Yes,' replied Garrett, 'but come with your hands up.' 'Oh, you go to h——l, won't you? You old long-legged s—n of a b——h!'

You see they were without fire, water or provisions, consequently we had the advantage. We had a good fire out behind one of the knolls and would take turns about, during the day and coming night, going to warm.

They held out until next day, when they surrendered, after being promised protection from mob violence. Kid was the last man to come out with his hands up. He said he would have starved to death before surrendering if the rest had stayed with him."

Chambers, after finishing gave a heavy sigh and wondered whether Garrett and Stuart would act white and whack up the reward evenly among the whole outfit, or not.

"Bob" and I made arrangements with the boys to loan us their part of the reward, which would amount to considerable over a hundred dollars apiece, until we got back to the ranch, to pay our debts with.

## 23. A TRIP TO THE RIO GRANDE ON A MULE

ABOUT the time we were getting out of patience waiting, the two boys, East and Emory, arrived with the good news that Stuart would be along in a few days, he having to remain over to get their part of the reward, etc.

Stuart arrived finally; he came in a buggy with a gentleman from "Vegas." His orders to Roberson and Torry's men were: "Boys, you fellows pull right back to the ranch, as I have got some important business to look after in 'Vegas.' We can come back after those cattle in the spring," etc.

The boys who had helped capture the "Kid" and outfit rounded him up for their part of the reward, but he said it was already spent. Oh no, they wasn't mad! Some of them swore that he would be a corpse before morning. But luckily for him he pulled for "Vegas" that night. I am not certain whether he was aware of his danger or not, but there is one thing I am certain of and that is, it wouldn't have been healthy for him to remain in that locality very long. "Bob" had even consented to the crowd hanging him. I was the only one who protested, for the simple reason that I do not believe in mob law. Of course I thought it very wrong in swindling the boys out of equal share

141

of the reward, after they had shared equally in the danger and hardships.

"Bob" was in a bad fix, in debt, no money and ordered home, by one whose orders his boss had told him to obey. The question was, how to stand his creditors off and get grub, corn, etc. enough to last him home.

I finally came to his rescue. As I intended remaining, I went to the merchants and told them his fix and guaranteed that he would send the money he owed as soon as he got home, or else I would let them take it out of my four mules and wagon, which were worth a thousand dollars at least.

They let him off; also let him have grub, corn, etc. enough to last him home, which would take fifteen days to make the trip.

As some of my boys became homesick, on seeing Roberson's outfit getting ready to pull back and as I was anxious to cut down expenses, knowing that I would have to lay there the rest of the winter, waiting for money to pay up my bills before the merchants would let me move my wagon, I let three of them go along with "Bob." Those three were James East, Cal. Pope and Lee Hall. "Bob" let Tom Emory, one of his men, who was stuck on the light mountain air of New Mexico remain with me. This left me there with a cook and three warriors, Emory, Chambers and "Big-foot" Wallace.

Just as soon as "Bob" had pulled out, I moved into town and rented a house, so that we could put on style, while waiting for the money I had written to the ranch for.

The mails were so irregular, on account of the deep snow which lay on the ground up there in the mountains nearly all winter, that I didn't get a letter from Moore for three weeks. In the letter were drafts for three hundred dollars; and Moore stated that I had done just right by not taking Stuart's advice and coming home. He also reminded me that I mustn't come back until I got the cattle, if it took two years; and also that I must scour out the Sand hills on the Plains around Las Potales, "Kid's" den, on my return. I distributed the three hundred dollars among my creditors and then wrote back to the ranch for some more, as that was already gone, etc.

We found the citizens of White Oaks to be sociable and kind; and everything went on lovely with the exception of a shooting scrape between a School teacher and "Big foot."

About the last of February I received another three hundred dollars and I then struck out, accompanied by Tom Emory, to hunt the noted Pat Cohglin and find out if he would let us have the cattle without bloodshed or not. As he had a slaughter house in Fort Stanton I struck out for there first.

We left the "Oaks" one morning early, Emory mounted on his pet "Grey" and I on one of the fat work mules and arrived in "Stanton" about sundown.

We rode up to Cohglin's slaughter pen the first thing and found a man by the name of Peppen in charge. On examining the hides which hung on the fence we found five bearing the "L. X." brand. I laid them to one side and next morning brought two men Crawford and Hurly, down from the Post to witness the brands. I then told Mr. Peppen, or "Old Pap" as he was called, not to butcher any more of those cattle sold by "Billy the Kid." He promised he wouldn't unless he got new orders from Cohglin.

From there we pulled for Tulerosa where Cohglin lived. The first night out we stopped at the Mescalero Apache Indian Agency, which is known as South Fork. There I learned from the store-keeper of a bunch of eight hundred cattle having passed there in a terrible hurry, about three weeks before, going west. He said that they were undoubtedly stolen cattle, for they drove night and day through the deep snow. I came to the conclusion that maybe it was Tom Cooper, one of "Kid's" right-hand bowers

143

with a stolen herd of Panhandle cattle, so made up my mind to keep on his trail.

We rode into Tulerosa the next evening about sundown. A young man from the Panhandle, by the name of Sam Coleman, who was on his way to Willcox, Arizona, was with us. We found the town to be a genuine mexican "Plaza" of about one thousand souls. We put up for the night at Cohglin's store and learned from the clerk, Morris, that the "King of Tulerosa," as Cohglin was called, was down on the Rio Grande on trail of a bunch of cattle stolen from him by Tom Cooper. I put that down as a very thin yarn, having reasons to believe that he and Cooper stood in with one another. I made up my mind that it was our cattle he was trying to get away with, after hearing of us being in the "Oaks."

The clerk had told the truth though, for he *was* after Cooper. The way it happened, Cohglin had only paid Cooper and the "Kid" half down on the last bunch of Panhandle cattle he bought from them and Cooper hearing of "Kid's" capture and of us being in the "Oaks" on our way after the cattle, came onto Cohglin for the rest of the money so he could leave the country. On being refused he got his crowd together and stole three hundred head of the latter's best cattle and pulled for Arizona with them.

After supper Emory and Coleman went to bed while I struck out to a mexican dance, at the outskirts of town, to keep my ears open for news connected with Panhandle cattle, etc.

There being plenty of wine, or "mescal," on the ground the "Greasers" began feeling pretty good about midnight. Of course I had to join in their sports, so as to keep on the good side of them. There was only one American in the crowd, besides myself.

I became pretty intimate with one old fellow of whom I made scores of inquiries in regard to Mr. Cohglin and the herd—the one I heard about at South Fork—that had passed there a few weeks before.

He knew nothing of the herd, no further than having seen it, but he pointed out a long-haired "Greaser," who was three sheets in the wind and swinging his pistol around on his fore-finger, who could tell me all about it, as he had piloted it through San Augustine Pass.

I learned that the herd was owned by Charlie Slaughter and that their destination was the Heeley River, near Tombstone, Arizona.

Marking out a lot of brands which I had never heard of on a piece of paper, I asked the long-haired fellow if he noticed any of them on the cattle. He did not. So I then marked off a lot of Panhandle brands. He picked out several, the "L. X." among them, this time, that he remembered of seeing in the herd. This satisfied me that the herd would bear inspection.

The next morning I told Emory what the old mexican had said and that my intentions were to kill two birds with one stone; find Cohglin and then follow the herd.

This didn't impress Emory very favorably. He advised me to return and get the wagon and outfit. I couldn't see the point, for we would lose at least a week by the operation. He took the back track while I continued single handed, accompanied by Sam Coleman, whose route was the same as mine until arriving on the Rio Grande, where he would change his course to south-ward.

# 24. WAYLAID BY UNKNOWN PARTIES

AFTER leaving Tulerosa our route lay across a young desert, called the "White Sands," a distance of sixty miles. That night Sam and I camped at a lonely spot called "White Water," where there wasn't a stick of wood in sight. We had to make a fire out of a bush called the "oil weed" to keep warm by.

The next night we put up with an old man by the name of Shedd, who kept a ranch on the east side of Osscuro mountains, near San Augustine Pass.

On arriving in the Pass next morning, on our way to Las Cruces, we could see the whole Rio Grande valley, dotted with green fields, for at least a hundred miles up and down. And by looking over our shoulder, in the direction we had come, we could see the white looking plain or desert, which extends for two hundred miles north and south. It was indeed a beautiful sight, to one who had just come from a snowy country, and we were loath to leave the spot.

Arriving in Las Cruces, (City of the Crosses) on the Rio Grande, twenty-five miles from Shedd's where we had left that morning, I went to making inquiries about Mr. Pat. Cohglin's whereabouts. I found out by the Postmaster, Cunnifee, who was an intimate friend of his that he was in El Paso, Texas, fifty miles below, and would be up to "Cruces" the next day.

That night Sam and I proceeded to take in the town, which was booming, on account of the A. T. and S. F. R. R. being only forty miles above, and on its way down the river to El Paso.

The next morning Sam bid me adieu and struck out on his journey for Willcox, Arizona, about two hundred miles distant.

That evening Mr. Cohglin, whom I found to be a large, portly looking half-breed Irishman, drove up to Mr. Cunnifee's store in a buggy drawn by a fine pair of black horses.

I introduced myself as having been sent from the Panhandle after the cattle he had purchased from the "Kid." He at first said I couldn't have them, but finally changed his tone, when I told him that I had a crowd at White Oaks, and that my instructions were to take them by force if I couldn't secure them in any other way.

He then began giving me "taffy," as I learned afterwards. He promised faithfully that, as he didn't like to have his whole herd, which was scattered through the whole White Mountain district, disturbed at that season of the year, if I would wait until the first of April, at which time the new grass would be up, he would help me round-up every hoof of Panhandle cattle on his range. I agreed to do so providing he would promise not to have any more of them butchered at "Stanton."

The old fellow was worried considerably about the three hundred head of cattle Cooper had stolen from him. He told me about having followed him with a crowd of mexicans into the Black Range, near the Arizona line, where he succeeded in getting back a few of the broken-down ones.

There being a fellow by the name of "Hurricane Bill," of Ft. Griffin, Texas notoriety, in town, direct from Tombstone, Ari-

147

zona, I concluded to lay over a few days and "play in" with him and his gang of four or five, in hopes of learning something about Slaughter and his herd, the one I was on trail of.

I went under an assumed name and told them that I was on the "dodge" for a crime committed in Southern Texas.

I found out all about their future plans from one of the gang, by the name of Johnson, who seemed to be more talkative than the rest. He said they were waiting for the railroad to get to El Paso; and then they were going into the butchering business on a large scale. He wanted me to join them; and said the danger wouldn't be very great, as they intended stealing the cattle mostly from ignorant mexicans.

One morning while Johnson and I were eating breakfast at a restaurant a man sat down at the same table and, recognizing me, said: "Hello," calling me by name; "where did you come from?" He then continued; although I winked at him several times to keep still, "So you fellows succeeded in capturing Billy the Kid, did you?" etc.

Johnson gave a savage glance at me as much as to say: d——m you, you have been trying to work us, have you? I kept my hand near old colts "45" for I expected, from his nervous actions, for him to make a break of some kind. He finally got up and walked out without saying a word. This man who had so suddenly bursted our friendship was a friend of Frank Stuart's and had met me in Las Vegas, with his chum, Stuart.

I concluded it wouldn't be healthy for me to remain there till after dark, nor to undertake the trip to Tombstone, for I had manifested such an interest in the Slaughter herd, etc., that they might follow me up, on hearing that I had left town. So I wrote a letter to Mr. Moore, telling him of the whole circumstances, and asking him if I had better take my men and follow the herd to the jumping-off place or not? I then struck back to White Oaks over the same route I had come.

148

That night I stopped at Shedd's ranch; and so did Cohglin, he being on his way back to Tulerosa.

The next day I rode the entire sixty miles, across the "white sands," and landed in Tulerosa about a half hour behind Cohglin and his fast steppers. I was tired though, and swore off ever riding another mule on a long trip. I had figured on being in mountains all the time, where I would have lots of climbing to do, is why I rode the mule instead of a horse.

The next morning I made up my mind that I would take a new route to the "Oaks" by going around the mountains through Mr. Cohglin's range which was on Three Rivers, twenty odd miles north. So before starting I inquired of Cohglin's clerk as to the best route, etc.

I stopped at the Cohglin ranch that night and was treated like a white head by Mr. Nesbeth and wife who took care of the ranch, that is, done the cooking, gardening, milking, etc. The herders, or cowboys, were all mexicans, with the exception of Bill Gentry, the boss, who was away at the time.

While getting ready to start for White Oaks next morning one of the eight or ten, mexicans, who were sitting on the fence sunning themselves, came to me, and told me of a near cut to the "Oaks," by taking an old Indian trail over the White Mountains, and advised me to take that route as I could save at least twenty miles, it being forty around by the road.

Mr. Nesbeth spoke up and said it would be better for me to travel on the road, even if it was further, as I might experience some difficulty in finding the old Indian trail, etc.

The "Greaser" then offered me his service, saying that he would go and put me on the trail so that it would be impossible for me to miss my way. I agreed, so he mounted a pony and we rode east up a rough canyon.

A ride of about five miles brought us to the almost obliterated trail. It lead up an awful brushy and rocky canyon towards the snowy crags of the White Mountain range.   149

About an hour after bidding the "Greaser" adieu, I came to where the trail made a short curve to the left, but I could tell from the lay of the ground that, by keeping straight ahead, I would strike it again. So I left it, and luckily for me that I did, for there was some one laying for me not far from there.

I hadn't gone but a rod or two when bang! bang! bang! went three shots in quick succession, not over fifty yards to the left; and at the same time my mule gave a lunge forward, on the ice-covered stones, and fell broad-side, throwing me over a precipice about eight feet to the bottom. My winchester and pistol both were hanging to the saddle-horn, but I managed to grab and pull the latter out of the scabbard as I went off, and took it with me.

The first thing I done on striking bottom was to hunt a hole. I found a nice little nook between two boulders and lay there with cocked pistol, expecting every second to see three Indians or "Greasers" peep over the ledge on the hunt for a dead "Gringo"—as the mexicans call an American.

After waiting a few minutes I became impatient and crawled on top of a small knoll and, on looking in the direction the shooting had come from, I got a faint glimpse of what I took to be two half-stooped human forms retreating, through the pinyon brush, at a lively gait. Suffice it to say I found my mule standing in a grove of trees, with his front feet fastened in the bridle-reins, about two hundred yards from where he fell. And between his forelegs, on the ground was a small pool of sparkling red blood, which had dripped from a slight bullet wound in his breast.

On examination I found that one bullet had cut a groove in the hind tree of my saddle, and another had plowed through a pair of blankets tied behind the saddle. I arrived in the Oaks on my almost broken-down mule about dark that night, after an absence of nearly two weeks.

## 25. LOST ON THE STAKED PLAINS

About a week after my return to White Oaks, I received a letter from Mr. Moore stating that I need not go to Arizona to look after the Slaughter herd as he had hired a United States Deputy Marshal by the name of John W. Poe, now Sheriff of Lincoln County, New Mexico, to go around by rail and tend to the matter. But when Poe arrived there the herd had been sold and driven to Old Mexico, so that we never knew whether there were any Panhandle cattle in it or not, except what I learned from the mexican, which appeared to me very good evidence, that there were.

On the tenth day of March, while taking it easy waiting for the first of April to arrive so that we could round up the Cohglin range according to agreement, I received a confidential letter from Mr. Geo. Nesbeth of the Cohglin ranch, giving me a broad hint that Mr. Cohglin was getting rid of our cattle as fast as possible, before the first of April should arrive.

The letter arrived in the evening and next morning I took "Big foot" along and struck out for "Stanton"—after giving Chambers and Emory orders to load up the wagon with grub and corn, and follow.

"Big-foot" and I arrived in the Post about three o'clock in the afternoon and went through the Cohglin slaughter pens, finding several freshly butchered "L. X." hides, which went to show that I had been duped, and that the hint from Nesbeth was true. We then rode down the "Bonetta" River nine miles to Lincoln, to go through the hides there and to look for a herd we expected the old fellow had hidden out somewhere along the river.

We stopped in "Stanton" that night and next morning struck out on the White Oaks road to meet the wagon and turn it towards Three Rivers.

We met the outfit at the mouth of Nogal canyon and camped for dinner.

It was sixty miles around by the road to Cohglin's ranch, the route the wagon would have to go and about twenty-five or thirty on a straight line over the White Mountains.

After dinner "Big-foot" and I struck out over the mountains, while Emory and Chambers went around by the road to pilot the cook, etc.

About twelve o'clock that night, after a very hard ride over one of the roughest strips of snow covered countries a man ever saw, we arrived at the Cohglin ranch.

We found the corral full of cattle, but, being very dark, couldn't tell whose they were.

Mr. and Mrs. Nesbeth got up out of bed and gave us a cold supper; and he also gave us a few pointers in regard to his employer's doings, etc. He informed me that Bill Gentry, the boss, had just began, that day, gathering the remaining Panhandle cattle, that might still be left on the range, to take to the "Stanton" slaughter pens. Hence those cattle in the corral.

After breakfast Gentry and his seven "Greasers" turned the herd out of the corral with the intention of keeping right on with his work. There was only five head of "L. X.'s," all large steers, in the bunch and I told Gentry that I would have to take charge of those and also gather up the rest that were on his range. He couldn't agree to that, he said, for his orders from Cohglin were, not to give up any of the Panhandle cattle, etc. I told him that I didn't care what his orders were, as I was bound to have the cattle.

Just about the time we were arguing the case the rest of my outfit hove in sight; they had been traveling all night.

After camping the wagon we all went out to the herd, which the mexicans were guarding and proceeded to cutting our five head out. Gentry tried to get me to wait until he could send for Cohglin, he having already dispatched a mexican to Tulerosa after him, but I wouldn't reason the matter at all, as I was mad about the way I had been served.

We went right to work after cutting out the five head, rounding up the whole range in search of more, but after three days hard work we only succeeded in finding three head more. But we left there with nine head, the ninth one being one of Cohglin's own steers which we butchered in the Oaks on our arrival back there, for the benefit of our many friends whom had been depending on us all winter for their fresh beef. Thus I had the satisfaction of getting even with the old fellow to the extent of one steer and a fat hog which we had butchered and stowed away in the wagon the night before leaving.

The mexican that Gentry sent to Tulerosa with the dispatch had to go on down to Las Cruces, on the Rio Grande, Cohglin having started down there the day before; hence we not having the old fellow to contend with.

After looking over the "Carezo" range, which was owned by Catron and Waltz and several small mexican ranges, we pulled into White Oaks with lots of experience but very few cattle.

On arriving in the "Oaks" I wrote to Mr. Moore telling him all about the way in which Cohglin had taken advantage of me, etc. Also advised him to have the old fellow prosecuted as I had sufficient evidence to send him to the "Pen," etc.

Mr. Moore on getting my letter, sent John Poe, the United States Deputy Marshal that he had sent to Tombstone, Arizona, over to have Cohglin arrested and put through the mill.

On leaving the "Oaks" for good, I bought a wagon load of corn, chuck, etc. for which I gave orders on the "L.X." company, not having any money left. The merchants had by this time, become acquainted with me, so that my name to an order was just the same as cash to them.

From the "Oaks" I pulled due east, around the "Capitan" mountains to Roswell on the Pecos River. I overhauled scores of little mexican ranches scattered through the mountains on my route, but failed to find any of our stock. At Roswell though we found two large steers which swelled our little herd to ten head.

From Roswell we went to John Chisholm's ranch on the head of South Spring River; and got there just in time as he was rigging up his outfit for spring work. They were going to start down the Reo Pecos to the Texas line, next day, to begin work and I concluded we had better work with them, in search of Panhandle cattle which might have drifted across the Plains.

I took my outfit back to Roswell, five miles, where I made arrangements with Capt. J. C. Lea, who kept a store, to board one of my men whom I wanted to leave there to take care of the ten head of steers until my return, not caring to drive them two hundred miles down the river and then back again.

Not having grub enough to last on the trip I bought a supply from the accommodating Capt. Lea, who took my note for pay. He also sold me two horses on the same terms.

We were absent two weeks on this trip, but failed to find any of our cattle. We came back with the satisfaction though of knowing that there wasn't any in that part of the world.

On our arrival back to Roswell we learned of the "Kid's" escape from Lincoln after having killed his two guards. That night Lon Chambers wore a different hat; he had swapped his star-spangled mexican sombraro off to one of Chisholm's men. This hat had been presented to Tom O'Phalliard by the "Kid," hence Chambers not wanting it in his possession for fear he might run across the "Kid." Chambers of course denied the above, saying that he never thought of such a thing, but traded it off just because it, being so heavy, made his head ache. But that was too thin we thought under the circumstances. Any of us would have done the same though, no doubt, knowing that the "Kid" had sworn vengeance against all of O'Phalliard's "murderers" as he termed them.

We found Emory and the ten steers doing finely. Tom hated to see us back for he was having such a soft time. All he had to do was turn the steers out of the corral, mornings, and then round-up and pen them at night again.

After drawing on the whole-souled Capt. Lea again for more grub, etc., we pulled up the Reo Pecos—looking through all the cattle on our route—to Ft. Sumner, a distance of one hundred miles.

We laid over in Sumner two days and went to a mexican fandango both nights, at the Maxwell mansion in which the "Kid" was killed shortly afterwards. The "Kid" was in the building while the dance was going on but we didn't know it at the time. The way I found it out, I had escorted a young woman, after the dance, one night, to her room, which was in the same building as the dance, and she bid me good night without asking me in. I thought it strange but never said anything. That fall when I came back there she explained matters, by saying that the "Kid" was in her room at the time, reading. I had noticed that she stood outside of the door until I had turned the corner out of sight. She also explained that: The "Kid" had the door locked and she had to give a private rap to get him to open it.

From Ft. Sumner we pulled due east on the Los Potales road, on our way to scour out the "Sand Hills" according to Moore's instruction in one of his letters to me at White Oaks. Before leaving the Post, the last settlement or store that we would come to before reaching the Canadian River, I sold one of the horses bought from Capt. Lea, for thirty-five dollars and laid in a small supply of grub with the money. Not being acquainted there my credit wasn't good, hence having to sell the horse.

Two days out from Ft. Sumner we came to the little rock house, at Stinking Springs, where the "Kid" and his companions held out so long without fire, food or water. Chambers and Emory of course had to explain and point out every place of interest, to "Big-foot Wallace," the mexican cook, Frank, or Francisco, and myself.

The second day after leaving Stinking Springs, we came to the "Kid's" noted "Castle" at Los Potales, on the western edge of the great "Llano Estacado."

Los Potales is a large alkali Lake, the water of which is unfit for man or beast. But on the north side of the lake is two nice, cool springs which gurgle forth from a bed of rock, near the foot of "Kid's" Castle—a small cave in the cliff. In front of the cave is a stone corral about fifty feet square; and above the cave on the level plain is several hitching posts. Outside of those things mentioned there is nothing but a level prairie just as far as the eye can reach.

We found about one hundred head of cattle, mostly from the Canadian River, but a few from as far north as Denver Col., at "Potales," which improved the appearance of our little herd considerably.

From there we went to the Coyote lake, twelve miles further east, where we found about fifty head more cattle, a mixed lot like the first. They were almost as wild as deer.

We then pulled into the Sand Hills, which extend over a scope of country from ten to fifty miles wide, and two hundred long—that is, two hundred miles north and south.

After about ten days hard work we came out onto the Plains again, our herd having increased to about twenty five hundred head. We were undoubtedly a worn-out crowd—horses and all. To do that amount of work we should have had at least five more men, and three or four more horses apiece. We only had one horse apiece, besides one extra, and the four work mules, which we had to press into double duty by using them to guard the cattle at night.

The next day about noon, after getting out of the Sand Hills, we came to a buffalo-hunter's camp on the head of Yellowhouse canyon, a tributary to the Brazos River. There was one man in camp, the other one being away on a hunt. Our cattle being nearly dead for water, there being none there, with the exception of a small spring, just large enough to allow one animal to drink at a time, I asked the hunter to give me directions to the nearest water from there, on our route.

Pointing to a cluster of sand hills about fifteen miles to the east, he said: "You will find Running Water, the head of Canyon Blanco, just eight miles east of those sand hills." As we learned, after it was too late, he should have said; eight miles *north* of the sand hills, instead of *east*. We were all acquainted with the country from Running Water north, but had never been south of it; hence us having to depend on the "locoed" buffalo-hunter's directions.

We camped for the night within a few miles of the sand hills. The cattle were restless all night, on account of being thirsty, which caused us all to lose sleep and rest.

The next morning, after eating a hasty breakfast, we let the moaning herd string out towards the big red sun which was just making its appearance.

Giving the boys orders to keep headed east, and telling the cook to follow behind the herd with his wagon, I struck out ahead on my tired and weak pony, Croppy, to find the water, which was "so near, and yet so far."

I rode about fifteen miles, and still no water. I then dismounted to wait for the herd to come in sight, but changed my notion and galloped on five miles further, thinking maybe the hunter might have meant eighteen miles instead of eight. The five miles was reached and still nothing but a dry, level plain, with no indications of water ahead, as far as I could see.

Thinking maybe I had bore too far to the south, I then rode five or six miles to the north, but with the same result. I then, after letting Croppy blow awhile started back towards the herd at a slow gait.

Finally a cloud of dust appeared, and shortly after, the herd hove in sight. The poor cattle were coming in a trot, their tongues hanging out a foot.

The way the boys cursed and abused that poor old hunter, at a distance, was a sin, after I had told them of our luck. Chambers wanted to go right back and eat the poor "locoed" human up alive without salt or pepper. But I pacified him by saying that maybe he had made a mistake of a few miles, meant eighty instead of eight. At any rate we continued right on, east.

About noon our ten-gallon keg run dry, and then we began to feel ticklish, scared, or whatever you wish to call it. But about three o'clock, we spied a bunch of mustangs off to the right, about five miles, and on galloping over to where they had been, before seeing me, I found a small pool of muddy rain water, which they had been wallowing in.

After letting Croppy fill up, and eating a drink of the muddy stuff myself, I struck back to let the other boys come on and fill up; also sent the cook to fill the keg, and to water his mules. I kept the herd, they being anxious to travel in search of water, pointed east, by myself, while the rest of the boys were absent.

We traveled till midnight and then pitched camp to get something to eat. After getting supper cooked, it was almost an impossibility to find time to eat it, as the herd kept milling and trotting around like so many crazy animals.

We remained there all night, and next morning used the last drop of water to make coffee. We found the keg, after draining it, to be about half full of solid mud.

I concluded that we had gone far enough east, so, that morning changed our course to north.

About eleven o'clock, while the hot June sun was coming down with vengeance, we struck a large lake about a mile wide. If ever a crowd was happy it was us. The poor cattle drank till some of them fell down and was unable to move.

We laid there resting up until the next day after dinner. Our grub had given out by this time, therefore we had nothing to eat but coffee and beef "straight."

When we left the lake our course was due north.

About noon the next day we came to the head of Canyon Blanco, twelve miles below Running Water, consequently we turned west, and traveled twelve miles up the dry canyon before pitching camp.

From there we turned due north again and traveled two days before striking any more water.

On arriving at Terra Blanco, fifty miles south of the Canadian river we struck Mr. Summerfield, and his outfit, from whom we borrowed grub enough to last us home. There were also two "L. X." boys in the Summerfield camp, and they, having five good horses apiece, divided with us. Our ponies were just about completely peetered out.

We landed at the "L. X." ranch on the 22nd day of June, with the herd of twenty-five hundred head of cattle, after having been absent just seven months, to a day.

## 26. A TRIP DOWN THE REO PECOS

O<small>N MY</small> return I found that the "L. X." ranch had changed bosses. Moore had quit and bought a ranch of his own, while John Hollicott, one of the old hands had been put in his place. Hence in the future I had to be governed by Mr. Hollicott's orders—that is while working around the ranch. One of the firm, Erskine Clement, had charge of outside matters, now, since Moore had left.

I put in the summer running a branding outfit, loafing around Tascosa, working up a cattle stealing case, etc., until the middle of October, when Clement received a letter from John Poe, who was prosecuting Cohglin, stating for Chambers and I to come over to Lincoln as witnesses in the Cohglin case. The time set for us to be there, was on the 7th day of November, therefore we had no time to lose, it being five hundred miles over there, by the shortest route.

Hollicott and Clement talked the matter over and concluded that I had better not come back until the next spring—"just put in the winter drifting over the country, wherever you can do the most good," was my orders.

Chambers and I struck out from Tascosa on the 22nd of October. He had only one horse, while I had two of the best animals on the ranch, Croppy and Buckshot.

We traveled up the river to Liberty, New Mexico, and from there cut across the Staked Plains to Ft. Sumner, on the Reo Pecos.

The distance from "Sumner" to the "Oaks" was about one hundred miles on a bee line across the country, while it was one hundred and fifty around by the road. We chose the former route, although we were told that there wasn't any water until reaching the Capitan mountains within thirty miles of the "Oaks." We both wished though, that we had followed the road, for, our progress being very slow on account of the loose dirt which would give away under a horse, allowing him to sink almost to his knees, we came very near perishing from thirst; and so did our poor horses.

We landed in White Oaks about noon of the fourth day out from Ft. Sumner; and had been on the road twelve days from Tascosa. We were welcomed back to the "Oaks" by all of our old acquaintances, especially those whom we had furnished with stolen beef all winter.

As we had five days to loaf in, before court set in, we went to work prospecting for gold, every body in the town being at fever heat over recent rich strikes.

The first day was spent in climbing to the top of Baxter mountain, where most of the rich mines were located, and back. The only thing we found of interest was a lot of genuine oyster shells imbedded in a large rock on the extreme top of the mountain. Of course this brought up a discussion as to how they came there. Chambers contended that they grew there during the flood, and I argued that they were there before God made the earth. We both finally got mad, each one, over the other's weak argument, and began to slide down hill towards

161

town, which looked something like a checker-board from where we were.

The next day we tied the pick and shovel behind our saddles and struck out on horseback to prospect in the valleys. At last we struck it, a fine gold bearing lead. It cropped out of the ground about a foot. I told Chambers to go to work and dig the prospect-hole, while I wrote out the location notices.

Finally an old miner by the name of Stone came to us. I was sitting under the shade of a pinyon tree writing, while Chambers was sweating like a "Nigger at election." "What are you fellows trying to do?" spoke up Mr. Stone, after grinning a few moments. We told him. He then said: "Why neither one of you fellows has got as much sense as a last year's bird's nest; that's nothing but a very common ledge of rock." We took him at his word and went back to town.

That night Mr. Stone gave us one of his mines, if we would sink a twenty foot shaft on it. We done so; that is, Chambers did, while I carried water, and rode into town every day at noon to bring him out his dinner.

Finally our time was out and we had to pull for Lincoln, a distance of thirty-five miles. Poe had written to me to come in after night, and on the sly, as he wanted to make Cohglin believe that we wouldn't be there to appear against him, so he would let his trial come off, instead of taking a change of venue. I left Croppy in a feed stable to be taken care of until my return.

Arriving in Lincoln, Poe sent us down the Reo Bonetta, twelve miles, to stop with a Mr. Cline, with whom he had made arrangements, until sent for.

Mr. Cline was a Dutchman who had married a mexican wife and had a house full of little half-breeds around him.

Time passed off very slowly to Chambers and I, although our host tried to amuse us by telling his hairbreadth escapes from wild indians and grizzly-bears.

We were indeed glad when Mr. Poe rode up, after we had been at the Cline ranch twelve days, and told us that we were free. Cohglin had "smelled a mice" and taken a change of venue to Mesilla, in Dona Anna County.

Before leaving Lincoln I had to sign a five hundred dollar bond for my appearance in Mesilla, as a witness against Cohglin, on the first Monday in April, 1882, which was the following spring. Mr. Chambers being sworn and not knowing anything of importance, was allowed to return home. We both received ninety dollars apiece, for mileage and witness fees.

Returning to White Oaks, Chambers remained there a week, making love to his mexican widow, and then struck for the "L. X." ranch, by way of Anton Chico, and down the Canadian River. The route he and I had come was too far between ranches for him, traveling alone.

I remained in the "Oaks" about a week after my "pard" had left, waiting for some more money which I had written for.

From the "Oaks" I went to Roswell on the Reo Pecos, a distance of one hundred and twenty-five miles, by the route I took. There I struck company, a jovial old soul by the name of "Ash" Upson, who was just starting to the Texas Pacific Railroad, two hundred miles down the river, to meet Pat. Garrett, who had written to come there after him, in a buggy. Ash was making his home at Garrett's ranch, a few miles from Roswell.

We laid over Christmas day at the mouth of Seven Rivers and helped kind Mrs. Jones, one of Mr. Upson's old-time friends, get away with a nice turkey dinner.

While sitting around our camp-fire at nights "Old" Ash would amuse me by relating circumstances connected with the "bloody Lincoln County war." He also gave me a full sketch of "Billy the Kid's" life, a subject which I am going to devote the next chapter to, as I imagine it will be interesting reading to some.

We arrived at Pecos Station, on the T. P. R. R., one afternoon about three o'clock. And it being a terribly lonesome place, we, after leaving our horses and things in care of an old wolf hunter who promised to see that the horses were well fed, boarded the west bound passenger train for Toyah, a distance of twenty-two miles.

We put up at the Alverado House, in Toyah. It was kept by a man named Newell, who had a pretty little fifteen-year old daughter, whose sparkling eyes were too much for me; to use a western phrase, she broke me all up on the first round.

After supper Ash went out to take in the town, while I remained in the office exchanging glances with Miss Bulah.

It was New Year's eve and Mr. and Mrs. Newell were making preparations for a ball to be given New Year's night.

Toyah was then one of those terrible wicked infant towns, it being only a few months old and contained over a dozen saloons and gambling halls.

About midnight Ash got through taking in the town and came back to the hotel. He was three sheets in the wind, but swore he hadn't drank anything but "Tom and Jerry."

The next morning the town was full of railroaders, they having come in to spend New Years. A grand shooting match for turkeys was advertised to come off at ten o'clock, and everybody, railroaders and all, were cleaning up their pistols, when Ash and I got up, we having slept till about nine o'clock.

Miss Bulah made a remark, in my presence, that she wished someone would win a fat turkey and give it to her. Now was my time to make a "mash," so I assured her that I would bring in a dozen or two and lay them at her feet.

When the shooting commenced I was on hand and secured the ticket which was marked number eleven. The tickets were sold at twenty-five cents apiece, and if you killed the bird, you were entitled to a free shot until you missed.

Mr. Miller, the Justice, was running the business for what money there was in it. He had sent to Dallas, six hundred miles east, after the turkeys, which had cost him three dollars apiece. Hence he had to regulate the distance and everything so that there would be considerable missing done.

Everything being ready, he placed the turkey in an iron box, with nothing but its head visible and then set the box thirty-five yards from the line. The shooting to be done with pistols "off hand."

Ten shots were fired and still Mr. turkey was casting shy glances towards the large crowd of several hundred men. Mr. Miller wore a pleasant smile, when he shouted number eleven.

I stepped forward trembling like an aspen leaf, for fear I would miss and thereby fail to win Miss Bulah's admiration. I was afraid, should the bullet miss its mark, that the few dozen birds would be all killed before my time would come around again, there being so many men waiting for a shot. At last I cut loose and off went the turkey's head, also Mr. Miller's happy smile. You see he lacked "two bits" of getting cost for the bird.

Another one was put up, and off went his head. This was too much for Mr. Miller, two birds already gone and only two dollars and "six bits" in the pot. He finally after humming and hawing awhile, said:

"Gentlemen, I don't like to weaken this early in the game, but you all know I have got a large family to support and consequently I will have to rule this young man out of the ring. He's too slick with a pistol to have around a game of this kind anyway."

I hated to quit of course, but it was best, for I might have missed the very next time, and as it was Bulah would think that I would have carried out my promise if I had been allowed to keep on.

After that, during my stay on the T.P.R.R., I was called

the "Turkey shooter." Often while riding near the railroad track, maybe four or five hundred miles from Toyah, some one would hail me from a passing train by that name; and whenever I would ride into a town there was sure to be some fellow on hand to point me out. They all knew me so well by my horse, Croppy, he being milk white and both ears being off close up to his head. He was indeed a notable animal, as well as a long, keen, good one.

That night nearly everybody got drunk, old Ash excepted of course, as he was already full. The ball was a grand success. The dancers on the womens' side, were all married ladies, with the exception of Miss Bulah and a Miss Lee; and those on the opposite side were a terribly mixed mob, but mostly gamblers, horse thieves and cow boys. The railroaders didn't take any stock in the ball. Maybe it was because there were so many on the floor wearing six-shooters and bowie knives around their waists.

It was indeed a grand sight next morning looking at black eyes and swollen heads. Every Chinaman, there being a dozen or two living in town, skipped for parts unknown that night. There was too many loose bullets flying through the air to suit them; and it is said that the "Pig-tails" have shunned Toyah ever since that New Year's night.

A few days after New Years a telegram came to Ash, from Garrett who had arrived at Pecos Station stating: "Come on the first train as I am in a hurry to get home." Ash got me to answer it as he, having drank too much Tom and Jerry, was unable to walk to the Telegraph office. I sent the following message: "Can't leave here; owe every man in town."

In a few minutes another one came, an answer to the one just sent, stating: "If you don't come down on the morning train I will strike out and leave you."

This one raised Ash's spunk, so he told me to write down
166

just what he told me, and then give it to the operator. I done as requested, which ran thus: "Go to, hic, h——l, d—— you!"

The next evening, Garrett arrived on the west bound passenger, and next morning, after paying a lot of saloon bills, etc., took old Ash back with him.

I had, the day after New Year's, went down to the Pecos and brought my ponies up to Toyah, therefore I took a little spin out into the country to pass off the time, every now and then, or at least to look through a few herds of cattle in that vicinity.

After spending about two weeks around Toyah, I struck out for Colorado City, two hundred miles east. Of course I hated to part with Miss Bulah; and so did Mr. Newell hate to part with me, for he was losing a good cash boarder.

## 27. A TRUE SKETCH OF "BILLY THE KID'S" LIFE

THE cut above was taken from a photograph and represents the "Kid" as he appeared before the artist after having just returned from a long, tiresome raid; and the following sketch of his short but eventful life was gleaned from himself, Ash Upson and others. The circumstance connected with his death I got from the lips of John W. Poe, who was with Garrett when he fired the fatal shot.

Billy Bonney, alias the "Kid" was born in New York City, November the 23rd, 1859; and at the age of ten he, in company with his mother and stepfather, Antrim, landed in the Territory of New Mexico.

Mr. Antrim, shortly after his arrival in the Territory opened up a restaurant in Santa Fe, the Capitol, and one of his boarders was the jovial old Ash Upson, my informant, who was then interested in a newspaper at that place.

168

Often when Ash was too busily engaged about his office to go to dinner, Mrs. Antrim would send it by her little merry-eyed boy, Billy, who was the pride of her life.

Finally Ash sold out and moved to Silver City, which was then booming on account of its rich mines. And it wasn't long until Mr. Antrim followed and opened up another eating house there, with Ash as a boarder again. Thus it will be seen that my informant was just the same as one of the family for quite a while.

The "Kid's" first man, as told to me by himself, was a negro soldier in Ft. Union, whom he shot in self-defence.

His next killing was a young blacksmith in Silver City whom he killed in a personal encounter, but not according to law, hence it was this scrape that first caused him to become an outcast; driven from pillar to post, out of reach of a kind mother's influence.

It was a cold stormy night when he, after kissing his mother's pale cheeks for the last time on this earth, rode out into the darkness, headed west for the wilds of Arizona, where he soon became an adept at cards and horse stealing.

He finally landed in the City of Chihuahua, Old Mexico, with a pocket full of Arizona gold. Here he led a gay life until one night when a bullet from his trusty revolver sent a rich mexican monte-dealer to his long and happy home.

The next we hear of him is in the friendly land of Texas, where he remained in retirement until the spring of 1876, when he drifted across the lonely Gandalupe mountains into Lincoln County, New Mexico, then the outlaw's Paradise.

At Lincoln, the county seat, he hired out as a cow boy to a young Englishman by the name of Tunstall.

In the spring of '78 Mr. Tunstall was killed by a mob, headed by a fellow named Morton, from the Reo Pecos.

The "Kid" hearing of his employer's foul murder, rode into

169

Lincoln from the Tunstall ranch to learn the full particulars concerning the killing. He and the young Englishman were warm friends and before leaving the ranch he swore vengeance against every one of the murderers.

Arriving in the mexican Plaza of Lincoln the "Kid" learned that Morton and crowd had pulled back to the Reo Pecos. So he joined a crowd composed of the following named parties: R. M. Bruer, J. G. Skurlock, Charlie Bowder, Henry Brown, Frank McNab, Fred Wayt, Sam Smith, Jim French, McClosky and Johnny Middleton, and started in pursuit. This was just the beginning of the "bloody Lincoln County war" which you have all read so much about. But it is said that the "Kid" killed every man connected with the murder of his friend before the war ended.

Billy was caught in a great many close places during the six month's bloody encounter, but always managed to escape, as though possessed of a charmed life. There is one of his hair-breadth escapes I wish to relate, just to show how cool he was in time of danger.

He and about a dozen of his men were housed up at lawyer McSween's in Lincoln, when thirty-five of the Seven River "warriors" and two companies of United States Soldiers under command of Col. Dudly of the Ninth Cavalry, surrounded and set the large two-story building on fire, determined to capture or kill the young outlaw.

The house was burning on the south side from whence the wind came, and as the fire advanced the little crowd would move further north, into an adjoining room. There was a fine piano in the parlor, the property of Mrs. McSween, who was absent, and on this the "Kid" played during the whole time, "just to amuse the crowd outside" he said.

Finally everything was wrapped in flames but the little kitchen which stood adjoining the main building on the north, but still the coarse music continued to sail forth out onto the night air.

At last the blaze began to stick its firey tongues into the kitchen. Then the music ceased, and the little band, headed by the "Kid" made a bold dash for liberty, amidst the thick shower of hot lead. The balance can be described best by quoting a negro soldier's words, he being nearest the kitchen door when the dash was made: "I jes' tell you white folkses dis nigger was for getting away from dah, kase dat Billy-goat was shooten wid a gun and two six-pistols all bofe at de same time."

The "Kid" and Tom O'Phalliard were the only ones who came out of this scrape unhurt. Mr. McSween, owner of the burned building was among the killed. He had nine bullets in his body.

Late that fall when the war had ended, "Kid" and the remainder of his little gang stole a bunch of horses from the Seven River warriors, whom they had just got through fighting with and drove them across the Plains to the Texas Panhandle, at Tascosa on the Canadian, where they were soon disposed of at good figures.

After lying around the little town of Tascosa for nearly a month, squandering their surplus wealth on poor whisky and mexican woman, they, with the exception of Fred Wayt and Henry Brown who struck east for the Chickisaw nation where the former's mother and two half-breed sisters lived, pulled back to Lincoln County, New Mexico, to continue their lawlessness.

From that time on, the "Kid" made a specialty of stealing cattle and horses, although he would kill a man now and then, for what he supposed to be a just cause. Let it be said right here that the "Kid" was not the cruel hearted wretch that he was pictured out to be in the scores of yellow-back novels, written about him. He was an outlaw and maybe a very wicked youth, but then he had some good qualities which, now that he is no more, he should be credited with. It has been said and written that he would just as soon shoot an innocent child as a mule-eared rabbit. Now this is all wrong, for he was noted as being kind to the weak and helpless; there is one case in particular which I can prove:

A man, now a highly respected citizen of White Oaks, was lying at the point of death in Ft. Sumner, without friends or money, and a stranger, when the "Kid," who had just come into town from one of his raids, went to his rescue, on hearing of his helpless condition; the sick man had been placed in an old out-house on a pile of sheep skins. The "Kid" hired a team and hauled him to Las Vegas, a distance of over a hundred miles, himself, where he could receive care and medical aid. He also paid the doctor and board bills for a month, besides putting a few dollars in money in the sick man's hand as he bid him good bye.

This circumstance was told to me by the sick man himself, who at the time was hale and hearty, on hearing of the "Kid's" death. While relating it the tears chased one another down his manly cheeks, to the end, at which time he pulled out a large red handkerchief and wiped them away.

After the "Kid's" capture at Stinking Springs, he was lodged in jail at Santa Fe, and the following spring taken to Mesilla, county seat of Dona Ana county, and tried before Judge Bristol for the murder of Sheriff Brady, during the Lincoln county war.

He was sentenced to be taken to Lincoln, and hung on the 13th day of May. On the 21st day of April he was turned over to Pat. Garrett, who, being sheriff, was to see that the law was carried out.

There being no jail in Lincoln, Garrett used his office, which was up-stairs in the two-story court house, to guard the prisoner in. Robert Ollinger and J. W. Bell, two men who should have been hung before William Bonney was born—judging from reliable reports, were secured to do the guarding.

The morning of April, 28th, Garrett was making preparations to go to White Oaks, when he told the guards to be very watchful as the prisoner, not having but a few more days to live, might make a desperate effort to escape.

Ollinger who hated the "Kid," they having fought against one another in the Lincoln County war, spoke up and said: "Don't worry Pat, we'll watch him like a goat." So saying he unlocked the armory, a small closet in the wall, and getting out his double-barrel shot gun, put eighteen buck-shot in each barrel. Then setting it back, remarked, at the same time glancing over in the opposite corner at the "Kid" who was sitting on a stool, shackled and hand-cuffed: "I bet the man that gets them will feel it!" The "Kid" gave one of his hopeful smiles and said: "You might be the one to get them yourself."

After Garrett left, the two guards had five more prisoners to look after. But they were allowed to wear their pistols, for fear of being mobbed by a crowd of Tulerosa mexicans who had chased them into Lincoln. They had given themselves up to Garrett more for protection than anything else. They had killed four Tulerosa mexicans, in a hand to hand fight, the day before, hence the mob being after them. One of those prisoners was a young Texan by the name of Chas. Wall, who had received two almost fatal bullet wounds in the fracas of the day before. It was from this young man, Mr. Wall, whom I became personally acquainted with afterwards, that I received my information from, in regard to the "Kid's" escape, etc.

About five o'clock, that evening, Ollinger took the armed prisoners across the street, to the hotel, to supper, leaving Bell to guard the "Kid."

According to what the "Kid" told after his escape, Bell became interested in a newspaper, and while thus engaged, he slipped one of his hand-cuffs, which he could have done long before if the right chance had been presented, and made a leap towards his guard, using the hand-cuff as a weapon.

Bell almost fainted on looking up from his paper. He broke for the door after receiving a stunning lick over the head with the hand-cuff. But the "Kid" was right at his heels; and when he got to the door and started down stairs the "Kid" reached forward and jerked the frightened man's pistol which still hung at his side, he having never made an effort to pull it. Bell fell dead out in the back yard, near the foot of the stairs, with a bullet hole through his body.

"Kid" then hobbled, or jumped, his legs being still shackled, to the armory and kicking the door open secured Ollinger's shot-gun, which contained the eighteen buck-shot in each barrel. Then springing to an open window, in an adjoining room, under which the other guard would have to come to get up stairs, he waited patiently for his "meat," as he termed it.

He hadn't waited long though when Ollinger, who had started on hearing the shooting, came trotting under the window. "Kid" called in a pleasant voice: "Hello, Bob!" Robert looked up, but just in time to receive eighteen buck-shot in his breast. The "Kid" then walked out onto the balcony, fronting on Main street, and emptied the other barrel into the dead body of Ollinger. Then breaking the gun in two over the balcony railing he threw the pieces at the corpse, saying: "Take that you s—— of a b——h! You will never follow me with that gun again!"

This proceeding was witnessed by nearly a hundred citizens, nearly all of whom sympathized with the "Kid," although they didn't approve of his lawbreaking. There was a few of his bitter enemies in town, though, but they soon hunted their holes, each one trying to pull the hole in after him, so as to be hid from the outside world.

After being supplied from the armory with a good winchester, two colts "45" pistols and four belts of cartridges, he ordered a file thrown up to him, which was done without ceremony; he also ordered the deputy County Clerk's pony and saddle brought out into the street, which was also done in double quick time.

The shackles being filed in two he danced around on the balcony quite a while, as though he was the happiest mortal on earth.

As he went to mount, the firey pony, which was being held out in the street, and which had once belonged to him, broke loose and ran back to the stable. But he was soon brought back, and this time held until the "Kid" was securely seated in the saddle.

After bidding everybody in sight adieu he rode slowly towards the setting sun, the winchester still gripped in his right hand. But when he arrived at the end of Main street he pulled off his hat, and waving it over his head, yelled at the top of his voice: "Three cheers for Billy the Kid!" Then putting spurs to the pony he dashed out of sight.

After traveling about four miles west he turned north-east, across the Capitan mountains, towards Ft. Sumner.

About the first of July, Garrett, who hadn't hunted much for the "Kid" since his escape, received a letter from a Mr. Brazil, who lived near Ft. Sumner, informing him of the "Kid's" presence in that vicinity.

Garrett after answering the letter, asking Mr. Brazil to meet him at a certain spot on a certain night, secured the services of John W. Poe, one of the whitest and bravest men in the Territory, and taking his Deputy, "Kip" McKinnie along, struck out for "Sumner" to capture the Kid if possible.

The little party of three arrived at the mouth of Tayban Arroyo, on the Reo Pecos, where Garrett had written Brazil to meet him, about dark on the night of July 13th. They waited there all night and Mr. Brazil failed to show up.

Mr. Poe being a stranger in that country, and not known in the Post, Garrett sent him to the town, a distance of five miles, to try and learn, by keeping his ears open and mouth shut, of the "Kid's" whereabouts, while he and "Kip" would meet him at "Sunny-side" a ranch seven miles above "Sumner."

About sundown Poe met his two companions, at Sunny-side, but was no wiser than when he had left them. Garrett then concluded that they would all ride into the town and if Peet Maxwell was at home he could maybe get some information from him.

Arriving in an old orchard back of the Maxwell mansion about ten o'clock that night, they tied their horses and crawled around to the front of the building.

There was a long porch on the south side of the house and about midway was Peet's room, the door of which opened onto the porch. Garrett knew where the room was, and there they headed for.

On arriving in the front yard opposite the door of Peet's room, which was wide open, the night being very hot, Garrett told his companions to lie flat down in the grass while he slipped into the room.

He found Peet asleep, but awakened him. He then laid down by the side of Peet, and they began talking.

Back of the Maxwell house was an adobe cabin in which lived an old mexican Peon. The mexican had gone to bed, and by a greasy looking table sat the "Kid," who had just come in from the hills. He had pulled off his boots to rest his tired feet, and was glancing over a newspaper.

Throwing down the paper he told the Peon to get up and cook him some supper, as he was very hungry. Being told that there was no meat in the house he picked up a butcher-knife which was lying on the table, and said: "I will go and get Peet to rustle me a piece." He started without either hat or boots.

176

While walking along on the porch, butcher-knife in hand, he discovered the two men out in the grass, and, drawing his pistol, asked in mexican: Quien es? Quien es? (Who's there? Who's there?) Not getting an answer, the boys thinking he was one of the Peons, he backed into the door of Peet's room, and then turning towards the bed, which was to the left of the door, he asked: "Peet, who is that out there?" Not receiving an answer again, and being suspicious of some one being in bed with Peet, he began backing towards the opposite side of the room, at the same time asking: "Who in the h——l is in here? Who in the h——l is in here?"

Peet whispered to Garrett: "That's him Pat." And by that time the "Kid" had backed until the light shone full upon him, through one of the south windows, giving Garrett a good chance to make a center shot.

Bang! Bang! went Garrett's pistol. The first bullet took effect in the "Kid's" heart, while the next one struck the ceiling.

The remains of what was once a fond mother's darling were buried next day in the old dilapidated Military Cemetery, without a murmur, except from one, a pretty young half-breed mexican damsel, whose tears, no doubt, has dampened the lonely grave more than once.

Thus ended the life of William H. Bonney, one of the coolest-headed, and most daring young outlaws that ever lived. He had dwelt upon this earth just 21 years, seven months and 21 days.

## 28. WRESTLING WITH A DOSE OF SMALL POX ON THE LLANO ESTICADO

AFTER leaving Toyah I followed the railroad east cross the Reo Pecos, out onto the Llano Esticado and through the sixty mile stretch of Sand Hills.

At Sand Hill Station, about midway through the sand hills, I left the railroad and branched off in a north-easterly direction in search of buffalo-hunter's camps. Knowing buffalo were getting scarce, and having heard of a great many hunters being in the vicinity of Ceader Lake, I thought it a good idea to go out there and see what kind of game they were killing. Being nearly south of the Canadian River country, I thought maybe they were killing cattle which had drifted down in there during the winters. But I was mistaken. I found their camps black with genuine buffalo hides. There being no ranches in that wild scope of country the buffalo, what few there were left, had nearly all congregated in there.

I played a single-handed game of freeze-out the first two nights after leaving the railroad, for there came a terrible snow storm,

178

which covered up the buffalo-chips, there being no wood in that whole country, so that I couldn't make a fire to warm by.

After striking the first buffalo-camp, then I was all right, for I could get directions how to find the next one, etc.

I finally, by circling around to the east, and then south, struck the railroad again, and landed in the town of Big Springs; where I was mistaken for a horse-thief, whom I answered the description of, and told to "skip" by one of my friends, a stranger who recognized me as the turkey shooter from Toyah. I didn't skip; and the thing was finally straightened up to their entire satisfaction.

I was out of money by this time, but found a draft in the express office awaiting me. Not having any particular use for the draft I swapped it off for a hundred dollars in money, to the express manager.

After looking through a few herds around the Springs I pulled north-east for the head of Colorado River, to take a look over the Lum Slaughter range, which extended from the head of Colorado River down to Colorado City on the railroad, a distance of about sixty miles. I went to all the sign camps, and also the head-quarter ranch, but didn't let my business, residence or name be known, which caused the boys to believe I was "on the dodge."

I rode into the lively little town of Colorado City one afternoon about four o'clock, and imagine my surprise at meeting Miss Bulah Newell on her way home from school. She and Mrs. Newell had left Toyah shortly after I did. They had left Mr. Newell at home to run the Hotel. And Mrs. Newell had accompanied Bulah to Colorado City, the nearest place where there was a school, so as to keep "the wild rattled-brain girl," as she called her, under her wing. They had rented a little cottage and were keeping house.

I ran out of money shortly after striking Colorado City, my

179

expenses being high, having to pay three dollars a day to keep my two horses at a feed stable, and one dollar and a half per day for my own board, lodging, etc., but found a good friend, Mr. Snyder, a merchant, who let me have all I wanted on my good looks until I could write to the ranch for some.

While waiting for an answer to my letter I would put in my spare time taking little spins out into the country, looking through herds of cattle, etc. The longest trip I made was three days, down on the Concho River, and that was just two days and a half longer than I cared to be away from Miss Bulah.

The mail finally brought two hundred dollars worth of "L. X." drafts, wrapped up in a letter from Mr. Erskine Clement, reminding me of the fact that his company wasn't a First National Bank. This of course was a hint for me to be more economical.

Having to be in Mesilla, New Mexico, a distance of five hundred and fifty miles, by the last of March, and wanting to look over some small cattle ranges on the route, I struck out. I hated to leave Colorado City on account of Bulah, but was anxious to leave on account of the small-pox beginning to spread there.

A forty-mile ride brought me to Big Springs, where I lay two days with a burning fever. The morning of the third day I pulled out, across the Staked Plains for the Reo Pecos, still feeling sick.

That night I stopped at one of the section houses, which were located every ten miles along the railroad. And the next morning after riding about five miles I became so sick that I had to dismount and lie down in the grass. After groaning and tumbling around about two hours I fell asleep.

About sundown an east bound freight train came along, which scared my ponies and awakened me. I felt terribly; my lips were parched, my bones ached and my tongue felt as though it was swollen out of shape. I started to lie down again, after the

180

noise from the passing train had died out, but there being an ugly looking black cloud in the north, which indicated a norther, I concluded to brace up and ride to the next section house, a distance of about five miles.

Arriving there, just as a cold norther was springing up, and riding up to the fence I called: "Hello!" in a feeble voice. A gentleman came out, and on informing him that I was sick, he told me to go in the house, that he would unsaddle and take care of my horses.

I walked into a large room where a nice blazing fire greeted my eyes. There was a lady sitting by the fire sewing. On looking up at me, as I stepped into the door, she gave a scream, which brought her husband in on the double quick. "Small-pox, small-pox," was all she could say. The gentleman looked at me and asked: "Are you from Colorado City?" "Yes," was my answer. "Well, you have got it, and I am sorry we can't keep you here to-night. I hate to turn a sick man out such a night as this, but I have got a wife and three little children here whose lives are at stake.

I had never thought of small-pox since leaving Colorado City, until the good lady put me in mind of it.

Oh, how my heart did ache at the thoughts of that dreadful disease, and having to go out into the cold night air. It was pitch dark and beginning to sleet when I mounted and struck out, west, aiming to go on to the next section house, ten miles, and try my luck there.

About half an hour after the light over my shoulder had disappeared I began to grow weaker, so much so that I could hardly sit on my saddle. So finally, dismounting, I unsaddled and staking the two hungry ponies out to a telegraph pole, rolled myself up in my blankets, my saddle for a pillow, and went to sleep.

I awakened just as day was breaking. The ground was covered

with snow, and I was almost frozen. I felt as though I had been sent for and couldn't go. My mouth, I could tell by feeling it, was covered with sores, in fact it was one solid scab, and so were my shoulders and back. Strange to say there wasn't a sore on any other part of my body. Those sores on my mouth was what attracted the lady's attention the evening before, although they had just began to show themselves then.

With great difficulty I saddled up and continued on towards the section house. This time I made up my mind not to let the folk's know where I was from, and if they had cheek enough to ask I intended to say Ft. Concho. To avoid the sores on my mouth being seen I tied a silk handkerchief around it. And should they ask any questions about that, I intended telling them I had some fever blisters on my mouth, etc.

I found only one man, the cook, at the Section house this time, the section hands having gone to work. I was treated like a white head by the cook, who no doubt took me for a desperado or horse-thief, by my looks. He thought no doubt the handkerchief was tied over my face to keep from being recognized.

I informed him that I was feeling bad and would like to lie down a few moments, etc. He led the way up stairs where the section hands slept and told me to occupy any of the dirty looking beds there. I laid down and told him to bring me up a cup of coffee. He brought up a good breakfast and after he left I undone the handkerchief and tried to eat, but couldn't, on account of my tongue being so badly swollen.

I found a looking glass in the room and took a squint at myself, and must say that I was indeed a frightful looking aspect, my face from nose to chin being a solid scab and terribly swollen. No wonder I frightened the lady so badly, I thought.

After drinking the hot cup of coffee I went down stairs, gave the cook a silver dollar for his kindness and pulled out. I was very anxious to get to a doctor, and Toyah was the nearest place to find one unless I turned back to Colorado City, which I hated to do on account of having to attend court in Mesilla, soon.

I arrived in Toyah about noon of the sixth day out from Big Springs. I headed straight for the Alverado House and who do you suppose was standing in the door when I rode up? Miss Bulah. The small pox had scared her and her mother away from Colorado City. The first thing she said was: "Hello, what's the matter with your face?" "Nothing but fever blisters," was my answer.

I didn't dismount, for fear of giving the pretty little miss the small pox, but rode a few blocks to Doctor Roberson's office, telling her that I was going after some fever medicine and would be back in a few minutes, etc.

The Doctor informed me that the danger was all over with, and that, if I hadn't been made of good stuff, I would have surely died, being exposed to bad weather, etc. He gave me some salve to dry up the sores, that being all there was to do at that stage of the disease, he said, and advised me to leave town, for said he: "If the citizens discover that you have had the small pox, they will have you taken to the pest house, where there are already three occupants, although the danger of it being catching from you is past." I assured him that I would fix it so they wouldn't find it out.

On arriving back to the Alverado House, my face still tied up, I hired a boy to take care of my ponies and then telling Miss Bulah that I wanted a room to myself, I went to bed.

Bulah would bring my meals into the room and sometimes sit down to wait until I got through eating, but I would never commence until she left. I would generally let her stay until she got ready to go, telling her that I wasn't hungry just then, but would try and eat it after awhile, etc. She would finally get tired and go, then I would lock the door and undo the handkerchief from my face. I kept this up a week, before eating my meals at the table with the rest of the boarders.

I finally struck out for El Paso, two hundred miles over a dry, waterless plain, and another hundred up the Rio Grande valley, making three hundred miles in all.

I hove in sight of the Rio Grande River one morning, but never got there until sundown.

When I arrived within a few miles of the river I noticed a covered wagon and what I supposed to be a camp, down the valley, about three miles out of my way. I finally concluded to turn off and go and stop with whoever they were for the night.

I found it to be a mexican camp, an old man, two boys and a grown girl. They had come from Larado and were on their way to El Paso. They gave me a hearty welcome.

Next morning about daylight I got up and went out to change Croppy, he having been staked and Buckshot hobbled the evening before, in a fresh place, but lo, and behold! there was nothing there but the stake.

I circled around and found both of the ponies tracks leading towards the river, a few hundred yards west, I followed, and found they had crossed over. After standing on the bank a few seconds, dreading to get wet, I went over too. The water was only about waist deep.

Near the water's edge on the other side I found some mocassin tracks in the soft sand. I could see through the whole thing then, from indications, etc.: two footmen, who wore mocassins, had stolen my horses and pulled into Old Mexico for safety. Where the tracks were visible in the sand, there was no doubt, they had dismounted and taken a farewell drink, or maybe filled a canteen, before leaving the river.

After following the trail, there being just the tracks of two horses, a few hundred yards out from the river I turned and went back to camp, to try and hire the old mexican's horse to follow them on.

The old fellow only had one pony, his team being oxen and

I had to talk like a Dutch uncle to get it, as he argued that I was liable to get killed and he lose the pony by the operation. I finally though put up the price of the horse as security and promised the old fellow ten dollars a day for the use of him, when I returned. This seemed to give satisfaction, even with the two boys who would have to hoof it after the oxen every morning, in case the pony never returned.

Just about sundown as I turned a sharp curve, near the top of the long chain of high mountains which run parallel with the river, I came in sight of both of my ponies staked to a pinyon tree, grazing.

I immediately rode out of sight, dismounted, tied my tired pony to a tree and crawled to the top of a knoll, where I could see the surounding country for half a mile around. But I couldn't see a living thing except the two horses, and the one I had just left.

Finally, bang!! went a shot, which sounded to be at least half a mile away, on the opposite side of the mountains.

Thinks I now there's either a ranch over there and the two thieves have walked to it, to keep from being seen with the horses, or else they have gone out hunting to kill something for supper. At any rate I took advantage of their absence and stole my ponies back. Near where they were tied was a small spring of cool water; the first water I had seen since leaving the river.

After taking a hasty drink myself, and letting the pony I was on, fill up, the other two not being dry, I took a straight shoot down grade, for the "eastern shores of the Rio Grande," a distance of about thirty-five miles. It was then nearly dark.

I arrived in camp next morning just as the big yellow sun was peeping over the top of the Sierra Blanco mountains; and the old mexican, who was awaiting my return, was glad to see me back.

That night I stopped with an old fat fellow by the name of

185

Chas. Willson, in the little town of Camp Rice, and the next night I put up in the beautiful town of San Elizario, which is situated in the centre of the garden spot of the whole Rio Grande valley.

The next morning I crossed the river into Old Mexico and took a three day's hunt through the mountains in search of a herd which had come from the north, and had crossed the river at San Elizario about a week before. I found it, but was unacquainted with any of the brands that the cattle wore. The herd had been stolen though, I think, from the way the men acted.

I finally landed in El Paso and found a letter in the Post Office from John Poe, written at Lincoln, New Mexico, advising me not to go to Mesilla until the day that Court set, as Cohglin, who was out on bond, was there and might have my light blown out, I being one of the main witnesses against him. Also, it had been reported that he had said he would give five thousand dollars to get me out of the way. He furthermore advised me in the letter to take the train from El Paso, as the old fellow might have some mexicans watching along the road for me.

## 29. IN LOVE WITH A MEXICAN GIRL

I FOUND El Paso, to be a red-hot town of about three thousand inhabitants. There were also about that number of people in Paso Del Norte, across the river in Old Mexico. I spent several days in each place.

I finally, after leaving my ponies in good hands, boarded one of the Atchison, Topeka and Santa Fe trains for Las Cruces, two and a half miles from Mesilla, the county seat.

There being better accommodations, in the way of Hotels, in "Cruces," nearly every one who was attending court would stop there and ride to the county seat in one of the "hacks" which made hourly trips between the two places. Consequently I put up at the Montezuma House, in Las Cruces.

There were several Lincoln County boys there when I arrived. Poe and Garrett came down next day. Mr. and Mrs. Nesbeth also came as witnesses against Cohglin. Mrs. Nesbeth had heard Mr. Cohglin make the contract with, "Billy the Kid," to buy all the stolen cattle he would bring to his ranch. But the good lady didn't live long afterwards, for she, her husband, a stranger, who was going from "Cruces" to Tulerosa with them, and a little girl whom they had adopted were all murdered by

187

unknown parties. Cohglin was accused of having the crime committed, but after fighting the case through the courts, he finally came clear.

A few days after my arrival in Las Cruces I went back to El Paso after my ponies. I ate dinner there and rode into Las Cruces about sundown. A pretty quick fifty-five mile ride, considering part of it being over a rough mountain road. The cause of my hurry was, we couldn't tell what minute the Cohglin case would be called up for trial.

I had a little love scrape while loafing in Las Cruces. I don't mention it because my love scrapes were so scarce, but because it was with a Mexican girl, and under curious circumstances, that is, the circumstances were curious from the fact that we became personally acquainted and never spoke to one another, except by signs, and through letters.

Her name was Magdalena Ochoa, niece to the rich Bankers Ochoa's in El Paso, Tucson, Arizona, and Chihuahua, Old Mexico, and she was sweet sixteen. She lived with her grandmother, whose residence was right straight across the street from the Montezuma Hotel, and who wouldn't let a young man, unless he was a Peon, come inside of her house. And she wouldn't let Magdalena go out of her sight, for fear she would let some of the young "Gringoes" make love to her.

I first saw her one Sunday morning when she and her grandmother were going to church. I was standing out in front of the Hotel hugging an awning post, and wishing that I had something more human-like to hug, when they passed within a few feet of me. The girl looked up, our eyes met, and such a pair of eyes I had never seen. They sparkled like diamonds, and were imbedded in as pretty a face as was ever moulded. Her form was perfection itself; she had only one drawback that I didn't like and that was her grandmother. I immediately unwound my arms from around the post and started to church too.

188

The church house was a very large building, and the altar was in one end. The couple I was following walked up near the altar and took a seat on the right hand side—on the dirt floor, there being no such thing as seats in the building—which was reserved for ladies, while the left hand side, of the narrow passage way, was for the men. I squatted myself down opposite the two, and every now and then the pretty little miss would cast sparks from her coal black eyes over towards me which would chill my very soul with delight.

When church was over I followed, to find out where she lived. I was exceedingly happy when I found she was a near neighbor to me, being only a few steps across the street.

I spent the rest of that day setting out under the awning in front of the Hotel, straining my eyes in hopes of getting a glimpse of her beautiful form through the large bay window which opened out from the nicely furnished parlor onto the street. But not a glimpse did I get. I retired that night with the vision of a lovely sunburnt angel floating before my eyes.

The next morning I went to Mesilla and answered to my name when it was called, by the Judge, and then told Poe that I had some very important business to attend to in "Cruces" and for him, in case the Cohglin case was called, to hire a man at my expense and send him after me.

On arriving back to the Hotel I took a seat in an old arm-chair under the awning. I was all alone, nearly every one being in Mesilla.

Finally Magdalena brought her sewing and sat down among the flowers in the bay window. It was indeed a lovely picture, and would have been a case of "love among the roses" if it hadn't been for her old grandparent, who every now and then appeared in the parlor.

At last I, having a good chance, no one being in sight but her and I, threw a kiss, to see how I stood in her estimation. She immediately darted out of sight, but soon re-appeared and peeping around a cluster of roses, returned the compliment. She then left the room and I never seen her again till after dinner.

I then started into the Hotel, but was detained by a voice calling, through the closed blinds of a window near by: "Me ketch you! Me ketch you!" Come to find out it was the proprietor's wife, Mrs. Duper, an old mexican lady, who had been watching our maneuvers. She then opened the blinds and asked me in broken English, what I was trying to do?

"Oh, nothing, much, just trying to catch on, is all;" was my answer.

The old lady then broke out in one of her jovial fits and said: "You ketch on? Me bet you ten tousand dollars you no ketch him!" She then went on and told me how closely the old lady "Grandma Ochoa" watched her young niece. In fact, she gave me the girl's history from the time of her birth: Her father and mother were both dead and she, being the only child, was worth over a million dollars, all in her own name. This of course was good news to me, as it gave my love a solid foundation, and spread a kind of gold-like lining over the young lady's beauty.

Finally, after court had been in session two weeks the Cohglin case was called up. His lawyers were Col. Rynerson and Thornton, while the Territory was represented by Newcomb, District Attorney, and A. J. Fountain whose services Poe had secured.

Mr. Cohglin began to grow restless, for the "Pen" stared him in the face. There were eight indictments against him, but the worst one was where he had butchered the cattle after being notified by me not to.

His only hopes now was to "sugar" the prosecuting Attorney, and that no doubt was easily done, or at least it would have looked easy to a man up a tree. You see Cohglin was worth at least a hundred thousand dollars, and therefore could well af-

190

ford to do a little sugaring, especially to keep out of the Penitentiary. At any rate whether the Attorney was bought off or not, the trial was put off, on account of illness on said Attorney's part, until the last days of court.

When the case came up again Mr. Prosecuting Attorney was confined to his room on account of a severe attack of cramp-colic. Judge Bristol was mad, and so was Poe. They could see through the whole thing now.

That night Cohglin made a proposition that he would plead guilty to buying stolen cattle knowing they were stolen, if the one case in which he had killed cattle after being notified not to, would be dismissed, or thrown entirely out of court.

It was finally decided to do that, as then he could be sued for damages, so the next day he plead guilty to the above charge, and was fined one hundred and fifty dollars besides costs.

Fountain, our lawyer then entered suit against him for ten thousand dollars damage.

I was then relieved. My mileage and witness fees amounted to something over a hundred dollars, this time. Of course that was appreciated as it was my own, over and above my wages. It came handy too as I was almost broke and needed it to take me home. I had spent all of my own money, besides nearly one hundred and fifty dollars borrowed from Poe.

It was the first day of May, I think, when I mounted Croppy in front of the Hotel, threw a farewell kiss at Miss Magdalena, who was standing in the bay-window, and started east, in company with Chas. Wall—the young man I mentioned as being a prisoner in Lincoln at the time of "Kid's" escape. I hated to part with the pleasant smiles of my little mexican sweetheart, but then it had to be done. I still hold a rose and a bundle of beautifully written letters to remember her by.

We stopped at San Augustine the first night out from "Cruces," and from there we struck south-east across the white sands

191

for the mouth of Dog canyon—the noted rendezvous of old Victoria and his band of blood-thirsty Apache's.

I had heard so much about this beautiful Dog canyon that I concluded to see it before going home, so that if it proved to be as represented I could secure it for a cattle ranch.

It was a ticklish job going there by ourselves, as a telegram was received in Las Cruces, the morning we left, that a band of Apache's had crossed the Rio Grande at Colorow, killing three men there, and were headed toward Dog canyon. But I had faith in Croppy and Buckshot, they being well rested and hog fat, carrying us out of danger should we come in contact with them.

We arrived at the noted canyon after being away from water nearly two days. It was a lovely place, at the foot of Gandalupe mountains.

After leaving there we went through the following towns: La Luz, Tulerosa, South Fork and Ft. Stanton.

At the last named place Charlie Wall left me, and I continued on alone.

I remained in White Oaks a few days, looking over my town property, I having bought some lots and built cabins thereon, and examining the "Old Panhandle Tiger" gold mine, the one Stone, Chambers and I owned. I had some of the rock assayed and it run twelve dollars in gold to the ton, besides a few ounces in silver and about two million dollars worth of hopes.

From White Oaks I went through Anton Chico, San Lorenzo, Liberty and Tascosa, and arrived at the "L. X." ranch after an absence of nearly eight months, and about a three thousand mile ride.

## 30. A SUDDEN LEAP FROM
## COW BOY TO MERCHANT

ABOUT the first of July, shortly after my return, Hollicott sent me to Kansas with a herd of eight hundred fat steers. My outfit consisted of a cook, chuck wagon, five riders, and six horses to the rider.

We arrived in Caldwell, Kansas, near the northern line of the Indian Territory, about September the first.

After putting the cattle aboard of the cars, and giving them a send-off towards Chicago, we all proceeded to take in the "Queen City off the Border," as Caldwell is called. I immediately fell in love with the town, also with a couple of young ladies, and therefore concluded to locate. I bought some lots and contracted a house built, with a view of going after mother.

I then struck out with my outfit to attend the fall round-ups in the vicinity of Camp Supply, Indian Territory. Returning to Caldwell the latter part of November, I boarded a train for Southern Texas, after mother, by way of Saint Louis to visit my sister whom I hadn't seen for thirteen long years.

I arrived in Saint Louis one evening—just in time to let an old flop-eared Jew take me in to the extent of a hundred dollars for a lot of snide jewelry and a Jim-Crow suit of clothes.

Not caring to hunt sister until morning I went to the Planter's House to put up for the night, and to note the change of twelve years.

After taking a bath and getting into my new rigging, I took a straight shoot for the office to make inquiries about the old boys. I found a long-legged youth behind the counter who, on asking how many of the old hands of twelve years ago were still there, pointed out Jimmy Byron, the kid I had the fight with, behind the cigar and news stand, across the hall. He was very busy at the time dishing out cigars, etc. to the scores of old fat roosters and lean dudes who were hurrying out after having eaten their supper.

The rush was finally over and then I made myself known. He was terribly glad, as well as surprised to see me. We had parted as enemies but now met as friends. He informed me that there wasn't but three, besides himself, of the old outfit left, and those were the old steward, who was now proprietor, "Old" Mike, who was still acting as night watchman, and Cunningham, the fellow who had slapped me and who was still clerk. The latter gentleman I didn't get to shake hands with as he failed to put in an appearance during my stay.

The next morning I struck out to hunt sister. I was armed with an old letter which gave the address, therefore had no trouble in finding her.

She was alone with her three pretty little girls, her husband having gone up town to his place of business—a drug store—when I found her.

The first thing she asked after kissing me, was, where I got my new suit?

Of course I had to acknowledge that I bought them from a Jew on Fourth street.

She then became frantic and wanted to know why in the world I didn't go to Humphry's and get them?

194

"Who in the dickens is Humphry?" I asked.

"Why, I thought everybody knew Mr. Humphry," she continued.

She took me up town to this great establishment of Humphry's that evening and there I learnt how badly I had been bitten by the Jew.

I remained in the city about a week and my brother-in-law spent most of his time showing me the sights.

Before taking the train for Texas I bought mother a trunk full of clothes, knowing that she would be in need of them after having "roughed it" for nearly eight years.

I stopped in Houston one day looking for Aunt Mary, but learnt finally that she had moved to the country.

I then took in Galveston and spent two days visiting Uncle Nick and Aunt Julia. From there I went to Indianola on a Morgan Steamship and became sea sick; Oh, Lord! I concluded I would prefer the hurricane deck of a spanish pony to that of a ship, every time.

In the town of Indianola I met a lot of my old Peninsula playmates, who were there from Matagorda, in their sail boats, with freight.

There being no boats down from Tresspalacious, I left my trunk to be shipped up the first chance and went to Matagorda with the two Williams' boys, Johnny and Jimmy. Nearly all the Peninsula folks lived in the vicinity of Matagorda now since the great storm of 1875, washed everything they had out into the Gulf, besides drowning about half of their number. Hence me going to Matagorda to visit them.

There were three Tresspalacious boys in Matagorda, and one of them, Jim Keller, loaned me his horse and saddle to ride home on.

Mother was happy when I told her to get ready and go to Kansas with me. There was only one thing she hated to leave behind, and that was her wood pile. She had spent the past two years lugging wood from along the creek and piling it up against her old shanty for "old age," she said. I suppose her idea in piling it against the house, on all sides, was to keep it from blowing over, should some kind of an animal accidently blow its breath against it.

After spending about a week, visiting friends and waiting for my trunk to arrive from Indianola, I struck out with mother for the enterprising State of Kansas.

I hired a neighbor, Mr. Cornelious, to take us to the Railroad, fifty miles north. He hauled us in an old go cart—one that had been sent from Germany in 1712—drawn by two brindle oxen.

We arrived in Caldwell a few days before Christmas and after getting mother established in her new house, I went to work for the "L. X." company again.

I had secured a winter's job from Mr. Beals before leaving therefore it was all ready for me to take charge of on my return. The job was feeding and taking care of about two hundred head of horses, at the company's ranch on the Territory line, near Caldwell.

Having lots of fat ponies to ride, I used to take a dash up town nearly every night to see how mother was getting along and to see my sweethearts. Thus the winter passed off pleasantly.

About the first of March I received orders from Mr. Beals, who was then at his home in Boston, Mass., to get everything in shape to start for the Panhandle at a moment's notice.

That very night, after those orders were received, I fell head over heels in love with a pretty little fifteen-year old, black-eyed miss, whom I accidently met. It was a genuine case of love at first sight. I wanted her, and wanted her badly, therefore I went to work with a brave heart and my face lined with brass. It required lots of brass too, as I had to do considerable figuring with the old gent, she being his only daughter.

196

Just three days after meeting we were engaged and at the end of the next three days we were made one. And three days later I was on my way to the Panhandle with an outfit of twenty-five men, one hundred horses and six wagons.

An eighteen day's drive, southwest, brought us to the "L. X." ranch. After laying there about a week, resting up, Hollicott sent me and my outfit south to attend the round ups in the Red River country.

We arrived back at the ranch about July the first, with three thousand head of "L. X." cattle which had drifted south during the past winter.

As I was anxious to get back to Kansas to see my wife and mother, Hollicott immediately gathered eight hundred fat shipping steers and started me.

I arrived in Caldwell September the first, and after shipping the herd, Mr. Beals ordered me to take the outfit back to the Panhandle and get another drove. This of course didn't suit, as I had only been at home a few days. But then what could I do? I hated to give up a good job, with no prospects of making a living by remaining in town.

I finally concluded to obey orders, so started the men and horses up the Territory line, while I and Sprague went to town with the wagon to load it with chuck. Mr. Beals had taken the train the day before to be absent quite a while. After getting the wagon loaded and ready to start, I suddenly swore off cow-punching and turned everything over to Mr. Sprague, who bossed the outfit back to the Panhandle.

The next day I rented a vacant room on Main street and, rolling up my sleeves and putting on a pair of suspenders, the first I had ever worn, started out as a merchant—on a six-bit scale. Thus one cow-puncher takes a sensible tumble and drops out of the ranks.

Now, dear reader in bidding you adieu, will say: should you

not be pleased with the substance of this *book,* I've got nothing to say in defence, as I gave you the best I had in my little shop, but before you criticise it from a literary standpoint, bear in mind that the writer had fits until he was ten years of age, and hasn't fully recovered from the effects.

FINIS

# ADDENDA

*Those wishing information as to profits and losses in the stock business as it is carried on at the present date, can find it—or at least part of it—in the following pages; and also a few words of advice to those wishing to seek work on the broad cattle ranges of the west*

## I

In Texas several years ago, the cost of raising a steer—no matter how old—was fifty cents, that being the cost of having him branded when a calf.

In those days men ran outfits, called "branding crowds," for the purpose of branding "mavricks" for themselves—and at the same time brand their *poor* neighbors' calves at fifty cents a head. In using the word poor, I mean men, or widows, not able to run a "crowd" of their own.

As a general thing the men who conducted those "branding crowds" used a forked pencil—that is, every time they branded a calf for a neighbor they would make a stroke in their day book with this double-geared money maker. The consequence would naturally be, that the poor widow, or crippled Rebel, would have a double number of calves to pay for about New Years. But then it turned out all right; as in after years the Eastern speculator, or "short horn," began to embark into the stock business with his eyes shut. That is, buying whole "brands" of cattle out according to the old books. For instance, if the aforesaid widow, or stove-up "Reb," could show up, and prove, that she or he had so many calves branded the *past* season, the buyer would pay for four times as many—that is, counting five head of cattle for every calf branded the year previous. Thus it will be seen that the forked pencil racket proved a blessing to the poor. The day though, of inveigling the eastern tenderfoot into paying for more than he really gets, is past, never more to return.

The cost of raising a three-year old steer on any of the great cattle ranges of the west can safely be put down at $4.75. That is, at the present time. Of course as time glides on and the humane feeling which now exists in the east shall invade the west, then the cost will be more, as the building of sheds, etc., for winter use, will be necessary.

To get that three-year old steer in Chicago, and a check or draft, for him, will cost $5.75, making the total cost $10.50. Now the average weight of a three-year old Texas grass fed steer on the Chicago market is 950 pounds. And the average price per pound, putting it at the lowest notch, is 3 cents, making the steer bring $28.50—leaving a net profit of $18.

## II

*Driving young steers "up the trail" and "wintering" them, as a money making scheme*

In south, or south-western Texas at the present time, you can buy two-year old steers for $10 a head. And to get them "up the trail" to any of the northern ranges, if an average sized herd, which is 2500, will cost $1 a head.

To "winter," or carry those steers over until the next shipping time, which is between June and October, will cost an additional $2. Now add the cost of landing them in Chicago, which I gave you above, also at the same weight and price as given above, and you have a net profit of $9.75 a head. The losses by death, theft, etc., are not included; but then you can safely put the losses "coming up the trail" at 2 per cent. providing of course that you use judgment in hiring experienced men, and buying good cow-ponies. And the losses during the winter from deaths—if you fed hay during stormy weather, which, by the way, was figured on when I put the cost of "wintering" at $2—and other causes would be about 1½ per cent.

Another class of trail steers are yearlings, which at the present time are worth in south and southwest Texas, $8 a head.

The cost of handling them is about the same as two-year olds. So counting $1 a head to drive them up the trail, $4 to "double winter" them—that is, carry them over *two* winters—and $5.75 to land them in Chicago, and you have a profit of $9.75—the same as for the two-year olds. The only difference is, you have had the *fun* of putting in two years with the yearlings, which is quite an item, providing you don't value time nor money, and like the business.

### III

*Starting into the cattle business with 100 head of two-year old heifers—what a young man of energy and bull dog grit can do in ten years*

Being a small bunch, it wouldn't pay to go to southern Texas, where cattle are cheap, to buy them, therefore you would have to pay about $15 a head for your one hundred two-year old cows, delivered to you. By the way, those same animals would cost you $10 a head in southern Texas, and if a good sized herd, another $1 bill per head to land them on your ranch—a saving of $4 a head, if able to start on a large scale; or lucky enough to strike a party who would let you drive in with them. Often you can strike just such chances, where a man is driving a large herd and will let you put your few head in with his—he paying you regular wages, and charging you so much a head for driving your cattle. By getting a chance like that your wages would almost pay the whole expense of getting your little bunch onto any of the middle or northern ranges.

After selecting your range, which, if you are a "tender-foot," should be as far as possible from a large cattle ranch, you should invest about $200 in four head of nice half-breed bulls—and another $200 in Spanish ponies, mostly young mares, so you could raise your own cow-ponies. My reason for advising you not to get near a large ranch is this: your cattle would be continually mixing up with your neighbors' herd, and there being so many, and scattered over so much territory, you couldn't keep track of them. Therefore a number of your calves would become "mavricks" and be eaten or branded by your generous cow-boy neighbors. If you understood the "ropes," and had the conscience, like your humble servant, it would pay you to get just as near as possible to one of those large English cattle syndicates, as then your herd would increase faster, and if you wished to sell out they would buy at good round figures to get rid of you.

An inexperienced man though starting in, I would advise locating, or buying out a water right, in the mountains of Colorado, Arizona, New Mexico or north-western Texas. As by so doing you could count every one of your cattle when they came into water. Whereas, on the ranges of the plains country you have the continual expense and bother of rounding-up, cutting out, etc., on account of them drifting during storms. In the mountains they find shelter and therefore don't drift much.

To begin now on your increase for ten years we will say that you began in the early spring. If so, you would brand 50 calves the coming fall.

The next fall you would brand 74 head; the next 96; and the fourth fall 108 head. Your next branding would be 135 head; the next 180. And still the next, which would be the seventh fall, 232 head. Another summer gone and 270 more frolicking calves in your herd. branding season is over again, and another 290 calves. The leaves are falling once more and your hot branding-iron has made 470 more little calves squirm. Now for the next branding, at which time you have been in the business a few months over ten years, of 624 calves. Thus your increase has run up to 2529 head. Half of those are steers which, if you have *used* *"blooded"* *bulls*, at average weight of 1000 pounds, and the average Chicago price, for that class of stock, of 4 cents per pound, would make them bring $40 a head.

Now, deduct the cost of raising those steers, $4.75 per head, and the cost of landing them in Chicago, $5.75 per head, and you have a net profit of $36,656. The steer calves of the last two brandings, of course wouldn't be marketable at the expiration of the time, but then we figured them *in* just to give you a rough guess of what your ten years' labor would amount to after all the steers had been sold.

Now, if you have used good judgment in securing your water right—that is, far enough from any other water so that you wouldn't be bothered with neighbors, and thereby have *grass* enough—you can imagine your future income on those 1264 head of she cattle—not counting what's left of your nest eggs, the first 100 head. You should also figure on the value of your stock of ponies, and the increased value of your ranch property.

In estimating the above I have figured on your putting up a few stacks of prairie hay—although you might not need it often; when you did, it would be like the Texan's pistol, you would need it like———.

## IV

*The cow-pony—and how he is abused on the large cattle ranches*

It requires at least five ponies to each man, on a large cattle ranch; on a small one, where the amount of work, such as rounding-up, cutting, etc. is less, the number can be cut down.

A cow boy should be allowed to keep the same ponies just as long as he remains on the ranch, as he becomes attached to them, and they to him.

If you want to see a cow boy on the war-path, and have him quit, just take away one of his good ponies. Of course, if he has got one that is "no good" he won't kick, as he thinks he might get a better one in its place.

A cow boy always has one or two, "cutting" horses in his "mount" which he uses only on special occasions—when he wants to "show off." Any of his ponies will do to "cut" cattle on, but this one he dotes on, is so much better than the rest that he keeps him fat and well rested for those special occasions.

To illustrate what the word "cutting" means, will try and explain:

After all the cattle in a radius of from ten to twenty miles are driven or run into one bunch, it is called a "round-up." I have seen as high as 50,000 head in one of those round-ups.

Now, we will say those 50,000 head belong to at least 50 different owners. And you being one of the owners and wanting to get your cattle home onto your own range you would have to put your men to work cutting them out—one at a time. Of course, once in a while a fellow gets a chance to "cut" two or three or half a dozen at a time—for instance, where a little bunch is standing on the outer edge, where you can dart in and "cut" them out before they realize what's up.

Now to begin, you will send about two men, on good "cutting" horses, into the round-up to begin "cutting" them out, while the rest of you help hold the round-up close together—or into a compact form—and keep the ones that are already "cut" out from getting back. The "cut" is watched, to keep it from getting too far off, by one man. The distance between the "cut" and round-up is from one to three hundred yards. About two *good* men on *quick* horses are generally placed between the "cut" and round-up, so that when the ones who are "cutting" runs an animal out *they* take it and keep it going until it reaches the "cut," or at least gets so near that it will go on of its own accord.

A "cutting" pony to be considered a "Joe-dandy" has to be awful quick as well as limber. An old experienced one can be guided with the little finger—that is, by holding the bridle-reins on the end of the little finger. While performing the "cutting" act he will move along as though half asleep, until the animal is near the outer edge, when all at once he will make a spring forward and take the steer or cow out at a break neck gait. No matter how the animal dodges in its mad effort to get back he will be right at its heels or side. Sometimes of course the best of "cutting" ponies will fail to bring the animal out—especially when tired or over heated, or when the animal gets on the war-path and goes to fighting.

The cow-pony is a terribly abused animal, especially in large outfits, where so many different men are at work. It requires treble the number of men on a cow-ranch in the summer that it does in winter, therefore it will be seen that most of the cow-ponies are subject to a new master every season, if not oftener.

For instance; a man goes to work on a large ranch, and is given five or six horses for his regular "mount." Maybe he has just hired for a few months, during the busiest part of the season, and therefore does not care to take the interest in the welfare of his ponies, as if he was going to remain for an indefinite period.

Now this man quits late in the fall, and his ponies are turned loose on the range to rustle a living as best they can until spring, at which time they are caught up again and given to some other new hand, who will put them through the same old mill again all summer.

To give you a faint idea of how some of the poor dumb brutes suffer, I will try and illustrate—that is, dear reader if you will let me use *you* a few moments:

Now to begin with; lean back, shut your eyes and imagine yourself an old knee-sprung, poor, sore-backed, pony, whose hips and shoulders are scarred up with spanish brands and spur gashes.

It is now early spring; the green grass is just beginning to show itself. You are feeling happy after your long rest, and the thoughts of having plenty of green, tender grass to eat, instead of having to root amongst the snow and ice for a few sprigs of dry tasteless herbs.

But your happiness is of short duration; for here comes a crowd of the "old" hands on their fat cornfed ponies to round you in; for spring work is about to commence. You break and run, to try and get away, but you are too weak; they soon overtake you, and start you towards the "home-ranch."

You are driven into the corral with the rest of your bony looking companions. The old last year's sore on your back has healed up and a new coat of hair is just starting to grow over it.

Here comes the boss down to the corral with a lot of new men he has hired for the summer. He is going down to give each man a "mount" out of the herd of extras, of which, patient reader, *you* are supposed to be one.

You are leaning against the fence scratching yourself when a rope is pitched over your head.

"Here 'Curly!' you can take this fellow for one of yours," yells the boss as he drags you towards the gate to meet "Curly," who is coming in a dog-trot to put *his* rope on you.

Now this man "Curly," your new master, has just returned from the east, where he has been spending the winter with the old folks, and telling the boys around town about the fun he had last summer on the staked plains, roping coyotes, etc. A couple of those "new" men who are standing at the gate, are old playmates whom he has persuaded to leave their happy homes and become cow boys too.

After each man has been supplied with a "mount," you are taken out, with the other four or five of "Curly's" ponies and turned loose in the "ramutha"—the herd of ponies which are to accompany the outfit on the "general round-up."

The outfit has now been on the road two days. They have been traveling hard to get to a certain place where all the different outfits, for a hundred miles, north, south, east and west, will meet on a certain day to begin "rounding up."

The place is reached about sundown. The little valley is dotted here and there with white-topped wagons—and still they come; wending their way down ravines from every quarter.

After supper the bosses all meet at one of the camps and lay out plans for work on the following day.

Next morning at the first peep of day everybody is eating breakfast, in all the different camps.

The morning meal being over, the "ramutha," which has been guarded all night, is driven up to camp and each man ropes the horse he wants for the days' work.

"Curly" catches you for the first time, since turning you loose in the "ramutha" before leaving the ranch.

When he goes to throw his old shell of a saddle on your back, you give a snort and go to pitching—like nearly all spanish ponies, after having rested a few months—which causes Mr. "Curly's" blood to become riled. So he, after you get your spree out, puts a hitch on your nose and begins to tame you, by beating you over the head and back with a doubled rope.

He finally gets you saddled, but when he goes to mount, you let in to pitching again. But he manages to stick onto you.

Everybody being in their saddles the boss tells "Bill," one of the old hands, to take "Curly," "Red Dick" and "Locoed Tom" (Locoed, meaning crazy) and drive down "San Pedro Canyon" to "Buzzard Flat" where the round-up will be.

So "Bill" dashes off on his corn-fed pony for the head of "San Pedro Canyon," a distance of twenty miles, with the other three boys right at his heels.

You finally step in a badger hole or stub your toe against a rock and fall, throwing Mr. "Curly" against the ground with a terrible force.

You jump up and stand trembling from the shock you received, while your mad master takes hold of the bridle-reins and goes to abusing you for falling—not only with his tongue, but by jerking the reins, which are attached to the severe spanish bit, causing your mouth to bleed, and kicking you in the stomach with the toe of his boot.

At last he is satisfied and mounts again, by which time the other boys are a mile or two off. Being such a common occurrence, when you fell they just glanced over their shoulders to see if "Curly" was killed or not. On seeing him jump up they knew he wasn't badly hurt. Hence them keeping right on.

Now you will have to do "some tall" running, under quirt and spur, to overtake the boys.

Finally the head of "San Pedro Canyon" is reached. Everybody dismounts to "fix" their saddles—that is, move them back in place and tighten the girths. "Bill" looks at his watch and finds that an hour and ten minutes has been spent in coming the twenty miles, over a rough and rocky country. Their ponies are white with sweat, and panting like lizards.

After surveying the surrounding country a few moments, "Bill" gives orders thusly: "Curly, you gallop over yonder," pointing to a large bunch of cattle five miles to the west, "and run those cattle down the Canyon; and you," talking to "Red Dick," "go after that little bunch yonder, while me and 'Locoed Tom' will push everything down the Canyon."

"Curly" starts off by burying both spurs deep into your already bloody sides.

When within half a mile of the cattle, they start at full speed, but in the wrong direction; hence you have got a three or four mile race, under quirt and spur, to run before they are "headed of" and turned down the Canyon.

After getting them turned, and to give them a good "send off," so they won't stop running until they strike the round-up, where men will be on hand to catch and hold them, "Curly" will fire his pistol a few times.

You are almost out of breath now, and should get time to blow awhile, but no, your cruel master, who feels good and wants exercise, after being housed up all winter, spies a coyote off in the distance and starts after it. He chases it five miles and then, after firing a few shots to scare it, starts back down the Canyon to help the other boys shove all the cattle down towards the round-up.

About eleven o'clock, the round-up, of several thousand head, is formed and ready for the "cutting" process.

Towards night the days' work is finished; the round-up is turned loose and each outfit starts to their respective camp with the little herd, which will be held night and day, and which will continue to grow larger every day, until too large to conveniently handle, when it will be sent by a few men back to the range, from whence they had drifted during the winter.

Camp is reached, and "Curly," in his great anxiety to get to the steaming "grub" or "chuck," which the cook has just taken from the fire, jerks the saddle off and turns you loose without washing your back—which should be done, especially in hot weather—at the same time giving you a kick with the toe of his number eight boot.

You are by this time a pitiful looking sight as you trot off towards the "ramutha." But the worst part of it is your back. The day has been very hot, causing the old last years's sore to become scalded; consequently, when the saddle was jerked off, the old scab with its new growth of hair, also went, having adhered to the blanket.

We will now drop the curtain a while, as our subject is not very pleasant to dwell upon.

It is morning; and the sun is just peeping over yonder tree-tops, which are alive with little birds whose sweet melodious songs make the air ring with joy.

But there is no joy nor happiness for you. It is your day to be ridden, therefore you are roped and dragged up to where "Curly's" saddle lies. The bridle is put onto you, and then your lazy master picks up the dirty, hard, saddle blankets—which have not been washed for a month—and throws them over your raw and swollen back. Now for the saddle, which causes you to squirm and twist; and then to add to the pain, imagine a man whose weight, counting pistol, leggings and all, is one hundred and seventy-five pounds, climbing onto that saddle.

You can now wake up, dear reader, for we know you are disgusted playing the role of a sore-backed spanish cow-pony.

But don't think for an instant that the majority of cow boys are the cruel-hearted wretches, such as we have pictured this man "Curly" to be. There are though, on every range a few who can discount my friend Mr. "Curly" for cruelty.

Many a christian-hearted boy have I seen quit and throw up a paying job rather than ride one of those poor sore-backed brutes.

There should be a law passed in the west making it a penitentiary offence for an owner, or head man of a ranch to allow, or rather compel, a man to ride one of their sore-backed ponies, especially after the sore becomes so large that the saddle won't cover it, as is often the case.


## V

*Wages paid to cow boys.—cost of a "cow-punchers" outfit, etc.*

A cow boys outfit is somewhat like a Boston dudes' rig, it can be bought for a small or large amount of money—according to the purchasers' means and inclinations.

If you wish to put on style, and at the same time have a serviceable outfit, you can invest $500.00 very handy; that is, by going or sending to Western Texas, or Old Mexico, the only places where such costly outfits are kept.

Your saddle would cost $100.00, although the Mexicans have them as high as $300.00. Another $50.00 for a gold mounted Mexican sombraro (hat). And $100.00 for a silver mounted bridle and spurs to match. Now a $50.00 saddle-blanket to match your saddle, and another $25.00 for a quirt and "Re-etta" (raw-hide rope). Your Colt's "45" pearl-handled gold mounted pistol would cost $50.00, a Winchester to match, $75.00; and $25.00 for a pair of Angora goat leggings, making a total of $475.00, leaving $25.00 out of the $500.00, to buy a spanish pony with.

Years ago costly outfits were worn by nearly all Cow-men, but at this day and age they are seldom indulged in, for the simple reason that now-a-days it requires more rough and tumble hard work than skill to command good wages on a cattle ranch. Cattle are becoming so tame, from being bred up with short horns, that it requires but very little skill and knowledge to be a cow boy. I believe the day is not far distant when cow boys will be armed with prod-poles—to punch the cattle out of their way—instead of fire-arms. Messrs. Colt and Winchester will then have to go out of business, or else emigrate to "Arkansaw" and open up prod-pole factories.

Well, now for the cost of a common outfit, with a few words of advice to the young "tenderfoot" who wishes to become a cow-boy.

Mount a railroad train and go to any of the large shipping or "cattle towns." Then purchase a cheap pony, for about $25.00; saddle for $25.00; leather leggings for $5.00; broad-brimmed white hat, $5.00; saddle blankets, which would do to sleep on also, $5.00. Another $5.00 bill for spurs, bridle, stakerope, etc. And now for the most important ornament, the old reliable Colt's "45" pistol, $12.00. If you are foolish enough to go without the latter, the cooks at the different ranches where you happen to stop will not respect you. Instead of putting the handle to your family name, they will call you the sore-footed kid, old man Nibbs, or some such names as those. We know from experience that the pistol carries much weight with it, and therefore especially advise the young "tenderfoot" to buy one, even if he has to ride barebacked, from not having money enough left to buy a saddle with.

Having your outfit all ready, the next thing to be done is, inquire the distance, north, south and west, to the nearest railroad from the town you are in. And which ever one is furthest, strike right out boldly for it. When you get about *half* way there, stop at the first ranch you come to, even if you have to work for your "chuck." The idea is to get just as far from a railroad as possible.

If you go to work for your "chuck," while doing so, work just as hard, and if anything a little harder than if you were getting wages—and at the same time acquire all the knowledge and information possible, on the art of running cattle. Finally one of the Cow Boys on the ranch will quit, or get killed, and you being on hand, will get his place. Or some of the neighboring ranchmen might run short of hands, and knowing of you being out of employment will send after you.

Your wages will be all the way from $15.00 up to $40.00 per month, according to latitude. The further north or northwest you are the higher your wages will be—although on the northern ranges your expenses are more than they would be further south, on account of requiring warmer clothing and bedding during the long and severe winters.

After you have mastered the cow business thoroughly—that is, learned how not to dread getting into mud up to your ears, jumping your horse into a swollen stream when the water is freezing, nor running your horse at full speed, trying to stop a stampeded herd, on a dark night, when your course has to be guided by the sound of the frightened steer's hoofs—you can command *good* wages, which will be from $25.00 to $60.00 per month, according to latitude as I said before.

If you are economical, you can save money very fast on the range, for your expenses, after your outfit is purchased, are very light—in fact almost nothing, if you don't use tobacco, gamble nor drink whiskey, when you strike a town.

There are some cattlemen who will let you invest your wages in cattle and keep them with theirs, at so much a head—about the average cost per head, per annum, of running the whole herd, which is a small fraction over $1.00.

# VI
*Average losses on a cattle ranch from deaths, theft, etc.*

The losses on a large ranch are more than on a small one; for the simple reason that the men who own the large ones are off spending their time and money in the eastern states or across the water; depending on the hired boss whose brain is over-taxed figuring on how to successfully take time by the fore-lock and make a stake of his own, while the small owner exhausts his time, brain and energy on the range, among the old, poor cows—trying to make them pull through the winter and raise another calf.

The average losses on a large cattle ranch, where the range is not overstocked, of course, can safely be put down at three per cent. And on small ranches about half of that amount. That will include losses from theft too—*now-a-days*, since the majority of people consider cattle stealing a crime.

Public opinion is causing lots of the old-time cow boys, or cow thieves, to select other occupations; for, while they remain on the range, it is hard for them to quit their old habits—which at one time were considered cute, as well as legitimate. Those who are slow to take a tumble, are fast landing up behind stone walls. The old-time cow boy will soon be like the buffalo and mustang, a thing of the past; although we predict that the former can be found in the city of Huntsville, in Texas, for a number of years to come. We know of several young, healthy ones, friends of ours, who are now residing there at the State's expense, and who are liable to live far into the next century, at which time the buffalo and mustang will have become extinct.

## VII
### *Raising cow ponies as a money-making business*

The cost of raising a three-year old gelding is not any greater than raising a steer of the same age. The only difference is, the former requires closer and better care.

For an example, we will take a young "tenderfoot" who has got a capital of $5000.00 to invest in the business.

He should go to south-western Texas as a starting point. There he could, by taking time, and leaving the rail-road towns, where horse buyers generally congregate, buy nice, picked three-year old mares for $15 a head.

Now, we will say you buy 110 head, counting the 10 head for losses on the trail, at a cost of $1,650.00. And six saddle ponies, for you and your two men to ride, until you can have some of the mares broken, at a cost of $150.00 making the total $1800.00. On passing through northern Texas, where the horses are bred up, you should also make a purchase of four young stallions, at a cost of $400.00; making your whole live stock expenditure foot up $2,200.00.

You should, before starting, hire an experienced horse-man— one who wanted a permanent job—to whom you would have to pay about $40 per month. And your other hired hand could just as well be a cheap boy, whose wages would not necessarily be over $15 per month.

You *could* use one of the saddle ponies for a pack animal, thereby doing away with the expense of buying a wagon, etc.; but in the long run, it would be best to buy a wagon and team, as you would need them around the ranch when you got located. The boy, or cheap hand, could drive the team, as his services would not be needed while on the move; for the only time you would need *him*, badly, would be while night-herding.

In selecting your range the idea would be to locate, or buy out, a homestead of 160 acres, encircling a spring or head of a creek, thereby giving you a water right for all time to come. The further from any other water the better, as then your range would be larger. For instance if the water was a spring, with water sufficient for three to five thousand head of stock, and no other "living" water nearer than twenty miles, you could count all the grass for ten miles around, yours. And another advantage in having such a range, you could count your stock every time they came to water; and besides they wouldn't be continually mixing up with other people's stock.

My advice, to a man hunting such a range as I have described above, would be to go either to the *mountains* of Colorado, New Mexico or Arizona. Of course there are fine ranges further north, but they are more suitable for maturing, than raising, stock.

The first thing to be done after settling on your new ranch would be to discharge your cheap hand, and thereby cut expenses down. And the next thing would be a log house, or dug-out, to live in, and a corral to pen your stock in at night until they became located. By having a corral, and the herd being small, you could save the trouble of night-herding. Of course after they become located you wouldn't have to watch them, either night or day.

Even if your water right has cost $1000.00, you ought to have enough left to keep your small expenses up until you had some three year-old geldings to sell. But if not, you could dispose of the six saddle-ponies, and ride mares.

Your increase, according to my figures, at the end of five years, counting on some mares not having colts, losses from death, etc., would be 700 head, half of which would be geldings, worth when three year-olds $30 unbroke or $40 broke. If sold while unbroke the whole bunch would net you $10,500.

Your herd would increase very fast the next five years. It takes at least that long to get a ranch on its feet. Besides the value of your range would be doubling itself every five years.

Of course you should put up some hay for winter use. If you did not need it, it would do for the next winter, if properly cured and stacked.

We will mention the fact again that the free and easy day of successfully raising stock in the wild and woolly west without winter feed, is past; and thank the Lord it is! For it is cruel letting stock starve to death.

From where I sit while penning these lines, on this first day of February, 1886, I can look to the southward, into the Indian Territory, and see thousands of poor dumb brutes marching up and down those cursed barbed-wire fences up to their knees in snow, with a blanket of ice an inch thick on their backs, the piercing north wind blowing forty miles an hour, and not a sprig of grass in sight.

Just think of it, ye cattle kings, while sitting in your city palaces roasting your shins before a blazing fire! But methinks you will be reminded of the fact next spring when you come out in your special car to attend the general round-ups. Dead cattle scattered over the range don't look very nice to the average eastern cattle king.

We think when you turn your faces towards the rising sun next fall you will know that there has been lots of hay put up—especially those on the Plains, or level ranges. From present indications and reports, this winter will cook the goose that has heretofore laid so many golden eggs.

*Adios Amegos*

DISCARD

BETHANY
DISCARD
LIBRARY